Kachinas & Ceremonial Dancers
in Zuni Mosaic Jewelry

Toshio Sei

Schiffer Publishing Ltd.
4880 Lower Valley Road • Atglen, PA 19310

Other Schiffer Books on Related Subjects:
Knifewing and Rainbow Man in Zuni Jewelry.
ISBN:978-0-7643-3548-8 $24.99
Hopi Bird and Sun Face in Zuni Jewelry.
ISBN:978-0-7643-3882-3 $24.99

Copyright © 2012 by Toshio Sei

Library of Congress Control Number: 2012949891

    All rights reserved. No part of this work may be reproduced or used in any form or by any means—graphic, electronic, or mechanical, including photocopying or information storage and retrieval systems—without written permission from the publisher.

    The scanning, uploading and distribution of this book or any part thereof via the Internet or via any other means without the permission of the publisher is illegal and punishable by law. Please purchase only authorized editions and do not participate in or encourage the electronic piracy of copyrighted materials.

    "Schiffer," "Schiffer Publishing, Ltd. & Design," and the "Design of pen and inkwell" are registered trademarks of Schiffer Publishing, Ltd.

Designed by Mark David Bowyer
Type set in Adobe Jenson / Zurich BT

ISBN: 978-0-7643-4167-0
Printed in China

Schiffer Books are available at special discounts for bulk purchases for sales promotions or premiums. Special editions, including personalized covers, corporate imprints, and excerpts can be created in large quantities for special needs. For more information contact the publisher.

Published by Schiffer Publishing, Ltd.
4880 Lower Valley Road
Atglen, PA 19310
Phone: (610) 593-1777; Fax: (610) 593-2002
E-mail: Info@schifferbooks.com

For the largest selection of fine reference books on this and related subjects, please visit our website at
www.schifferbooks.com
We are always looking for people to write books on new and related subjects. If you have an idea for a book, please contact us at proposals@schifferbooks.com

This book may be purchased from the publisher.
Please try your bookstore first.
You may also write for a free catalog.

In Europe, Schiffer books are distributed by
Bushwood Books
6 Marksbury Ave.
Kew Gardens
Surrey TW9 4JF England
Phone: 44 (0) 20 8392 8585; Fax: 44 (0) 20 8392 9876
E-mail: info@bushwoodbooks.co.uk
Website: www.bushwoodbooks.co.uk

Contents

Acknowledgments 6

Preface 8

Introduction 9
    The Origin of Kachina Jewelry 10
    Kachina Jewelry Artists in the C. G. Wallace Collection 11
    On the Taboo of Making Kachina Jewelry to Sell 13

I. Anna Rita, Lambert Homer, Jr., and Zuni Mosaic Artists in this Book 15
    Anna Rita and Lambert Homer, Jr. 15
    Edward and Madeline Beyuka 18
    Sybil Cachini 18
    Robert Cachini, Sr. 19
    Dexter Cellicion 19
    Andrew Dewa 19
    Theodore and Margaret Edaakie 19
    Anthony and Rita Edaakie 20
    Lambert Homer, Sr. 20
    Mary Kallestewa 20
    Curtis Kucate 21
    Morris "Red" Leekela 21
    Leonard Lonjose 21
    Mabel Lonjose 21
    John Lucio 21
    Vera Luna 22
    Leonard Martza 22
    Walter Nahktewa 22
    Tony Ohmsatte 22
    Quincy Peynetsa 23

    Augustine and Rosalie Pinto...23
    Ida Vacit Poblano...23
    Leo Poblano..24
    Elliott Qualo...24
    Ralph Quam...24
    Dixon and Martha Hustito Shebola..25
    Porfilio and Ann Sheyka..25
    Myra and Lee Tucson..25
    Frank Vacit...25
    Joe Zunie..26
    Lincoln and Helen Zunie...26
    William Zunie..26

II. Kachinas and Ceremonial Dancers..27
    Classification of Kachinas and Ceremonial Dancers..27
    Kachinas in Shalako Ceremony...27
    Shalako..29
    Saiyatasha..34
    Hututu...41
    Yamuhakto...42
    Shulawitsi...42
    Salimopia...45
    Koyemshi..45

III. Kachinas in the Corn Dance Ceremony...54
    Corn Dance, Rain Dance, and Other Ceremonies..54
    Kachinas in the Corn Dance Ceremony...54
    Antelope Kachina...54
    Ram Kachina...68
    Turkey Kachina...73
    Wotemthla Kachina...75
    Eagle Kachina...78
    Bear Kachina...82
    Comanche Kachina..82

IV. Kachinas in the Rain Dance and Other Ceremonies 87
- Kachinas in the Rain Dance Ceremony 87
- Downy Feathers Hanging Kachina 87
- Kokokshi 89
- Kachinas in Other Ceremonies 90

V. Dancers in the Social Dances 95
- Eagle Dancers 95
- Comanche Dancer 107
- Ralph Quam 110
- Buffalo Dancer 114
- Olla Maiden 118
- Other Dancers 121

VI. Kachinas and Ceremonial Dancers from Other Tribes 123
- Hopi Butterfly Maiden 123
- Hopi Snake Dancer 125
- Hopi Snake Dancer in Zuni Jewelry 126
- Apache Mountain Spirit Dancer 131
- Other Hopi Kachinas 141
- Ceremonial Dancer from Mexico 145

VII. Present Kachina Jewelry Artists 146
- Philander Gia 146
- Andrea Lonjose Shirley 151
- Eldred Martinez 155

Conclusion 157

References 158

Artist Index 160

Acknowledgments

Special thanks should first go to the Sheche family: Thelma, my closest friend in Zuni, her brother, Curtis Kucate, her son, Arden Kucate, and her daughter, Lorandina Sheche. They have accepted me as a family guest for more than 10 years and introduced me to other artists such as Rita Edaakie, Bessie Vacit, Sarah Leekya and Juana Homer. These artists further introduced me to their relatives such as Raphael Homer Jr., Anna Rita Homer, Raylan Edaakie and Bradley Edaakie. When I first began this project, Leonard Martza helped me identify artists who made certain older jewelry pieces I had owned. His older sister, Genevieve Tucson, taught me who Harry Deutsawe was and what kind of pieces he made. This book owes a lot to these generous artists.

My old friends and potters, Milford and Randy Nahohai, taught me where certain artists lived and drew me maps to find them. Without their help, I could not have visited and interviewed these artists. I always appreciated their hospitality and help.

After I published my first Zuni jewelry book, *Knifewing and Rainbow Man in Zuni Jewelry*, I became acquainted with Tom Kennedy, the director of the Zuni Tourism and Visitor Center. He helped me to have my collection show, book signing, and presentation concerning the book at the Visitor Center, where I met many wonderful Zuni people and artists including Dan Simplicio, Jr., Roger Tsabetsaye, and Marcus Peyketewa.

The director of A:shiwi A:wan Museum, Jim Enote, and I became friends through Facebook. He kindly invited me for dinner at his home and introduced me to one of the best needlepoint artists, Octavius Seowtewa, who helped me to attribute a ring to a particular artist. My heartfelt thanks go to these wonderful Zuni artists and people.

I have compiled my collection mainly through an internet auction site, where I transacted with the seller, Vickey Kohnke. She helped me identify the work of Anna Rita and Lambert Homer, Jr., through my son, Yuki. My appreciation should go to her. Perry Null of the Perry Null Trading Company in Gallup helped me to attribute three unidentified pieces to Red Leekela at the last moment. He is the final helper to me.

Lastly, without my wife Noriko's generous understanding of my passion for collecting, I could not compile my Zuni jewelry collection in this book. My daughter, Makiri, my son-in-law, Chad, and my son, Yuki, have helped me build this collection. Yuki helped me proofread my rough draft as well. Without their help, this book would not have become reality.

Preface

I have planned to write six books on older Zuni jewelry, which cover all ranges of designs and styles made from 1930s through 1960s. The main purpose of this project is to attribute each particular older jewelry piece to certain Zuni lapidaries/silversmiths and to confirm these attributions whenever possible by means of field research. However, it turned out to be very difficult and sometimes confusing because of conflicting attributions among my informants. Therefore, I have had to see spouses or children of attributed artists and ask whether or not they could confirm these attributions. Sometimes, this process was not possible, and some attributions remained hypotheses and were left for future study.

I published my fist book, *Knifewing and Rainbow Man in Zuni Jewelry*, in 2010, and the second book, *Hopi Bird and Sun Face* in 2012. This third book is solely on Kachinas and ceremonial dancers. Through the field research for this third book, I found Lambert Homer, Jr.'s wife, Anna Rita Homer, and confirmed their various designs. I also met a wonderful new Kachina jewelry artist, Philander Gia. This book introduces his marvelous works for the first time. It is my great honor to introduce these wonderful artists for the first time.

Introduction

C. G. Wallace is the single most influential person in the Zuni jewelry history. As Slaney (1998) noted,

> In a statement that emphasizes the dual but conflicting nature of his advice, "I never ceased them to impress on them that they should stay with tradition and unique pieces….Individuality and authenticity are what made Indian Jewelry valuable" (Vonier 1975).

He encouraged Zuni artists to stay with the traditional designs and, at the same time, to create their own unique version of the designs.

Thus, the Knifewing first appeared in jewelry for sale in 1928 and then was followed by Rainbow Man, Sun Face, and Hopi Bird/Thunderbird. They are authentic and not realistic. Because they are not the Kachinas in the stricter sense, almost all Zuni jewelers used these designs in their jewelry (Ostler et al., 1996, p. 88). Ostler and his colleagues describe them as follows:

> Knifewing is a mythological being with wings covered in flint blades who sweeps down from the sky and carries off beautiful Zuni girls. The Rainbow Man is associated with summer rains and the beautiful colors of the heavens. Neither of these figures are kachinas and, although important in Zuni traditions, do not have the same power as the kachinas. This may explain why jewelers used these beings in their work at first before venturing on to the more powerful and potentially controversial beings.

Bedinger (1973) notes that "[T]he Rainbow and Sun Gods were added to Knifewing, and other designs, described later, were used as time went on" (p.148).

King (1976) says that "[D]esign subjects for inlay in any material started with the Rainbow Man, Knifewing Warrior God, and Sun God in the early 1940's, then diversified to Kachinas and other religious concepts, and now include all sorts of human and animal figures, as well as a modicum of geometric motifs" (p.51).

Arizona Highways (January, 1945) also states that "[N]ot content with turquoise and silver, Zuni conceived the idea of fashioning the designs of their 'knifewing birds' and 'rainbow' gods into jewelry. The results were fantasies in design and color. These pieces are fashioned from making mosaics of turquoise, a form of native jet, white and pink abalone shell."

Thus, *Arizona Highways* (January, 1945) included Knifewing, Rainbow Man, and Butterfly designs. *Arizona Highways* (August, 1952) featured Knifewing, Rainbow Man, Butterfly, Sun Face, Hopi Bird, Hopi Maiden, Navajo Woman at her loom, deer, donkey and horse designs. *Arizona Highways* (August, 1959) first featured Kachina figures such as Long Horn, Long Hair, and Eagle Kachinas and Tablita Dancer, in addition to Knifewing, Rainbow Man, Sun face, Hopi Bird, horse and ox.

In this way, Knifewing came first, and, then, Rainbow Man, Sun Face, Hopi Bird/Thunderbird and butterfly joined the staples of the Zuni mosaic jewelry designs.

I concentrated solely on Knifewing and Rainbow Man designs in my first book and on Hopi Bird and Sun Face in the second. In this third book I am going to discuss the Kachina and Ceremonial Dancer designs made mainly in the 1940s-1960s. I will try to attribute many historical pieces to specific Zuni artists as clearly as possible. Through these processes, I would like to show again the inter-personal as well as intra-personal variation of pieces that Zuni artists made in the 1930s-1960s. In doing so, I hope we can appreciate the great tradition of the Zuni mosaic jewelry, Zuni people will feel greater pride in it, and Zuni jewelry artists will enrich the tradition further in the future.

The Origin of Kachina Jewelry

It is conceivable that Kachina jewelry depicting Kachinas and Ceremonial Dancers for religious use was made in the 1800s. As I described in my first book, the jewelry depicting the shield of the Priests of the Bow were made and presented to Frank Hamilton Kushing in the 1890s.

King (1976) cited C. G. Wallace's statement:

> "When I came to Zuni, the Dancers were bedecked with inlaid shell. Its use goes back to prehistoric times." (p.51)

Thus, it is probable that Kachina jewelry for religious or ceremonial use could be firmly founded by the 19th and the early 20th centuries. How about the origin of Kachina jewelry for sale?

On this matter, King noted that Wallace ordered Zuni artists to inlay silver before 1920.

Therefore, Kachina jewelry could be made before 1920. However, it is not certain whether this inlaying silver includes Kachina Jewelry.

The earliest Kachina jewelry in literature is the Eagle Kachina made by Bruce Zunie in 1925 (Ostler et al., 1996, p. 84). It is housed in the Heard Museum, so that this Eagle Kachina may formerly be a part of the C. G. Wallace collection. Wallace may have later donated this Kachina to the museum. Even if the first Kachina jewelry for sale was made in the mid-1920s, it does not necessarily mean Kachina jewelry was produced in quantity.

My examination of the *The C. G. Wallace Collection of American Indian Art* auction catalog revealed that Teddy Weahkee made a Hututu pin in 1930, Leo Poblano made a Long Horn figure in 1933, and Jerry Watson made a Fire God figure in 1935. These are the earliest Kachina jewelry in the catalogue, and the more than half Kachina jewelry are made in the 1940s.

Consequently, Kachina jewelry for sale in Zuni was made in quantity by as many as ten artists in the 1940s, although Kachina jewelry was made as early as the 1920s and 1930s.

Kachina Jewelry Artists in the C. G. Wallace Collection

In the *The C. G. Wallace Collection of American Indian Art* auction catalog, we find that 10 artists made Kachinas and Ceremonial Dancers in jewelry for sale (see table on page 12). Among these ten artists, Leo Poblano provided the highest number (seventeen pieces), and two of them are Hopi Maiden figures. Almost all Kachinas observed in the Shalako ceremony such as Shalako, Mud Head, Long Horn Kachina, Hututu, and Yamuhakto or Log Carrier Kachina represent the remaining 15 pieces. While the oldest one is Long Horn Kachina made in 1933 and the second oldest is Shalako made in 1939, most pieces are from the 1940s. For example, Poblano's famous Hopi Snake Dancer was made in 1945 after his marriage with Hopi artist, Daisy Hooee Nampeyo.

Leo Poblano

No.	Figure	Ht.	Date
#24	Yamuhakto (log carrier) figure	7.13	1942
#98	Hopi Maiden figure	6.25	1938
#99	Shalako figure	6.25	1939
#128	Mud Head figure	2.5	1942
#224	Plains Warrior figure	8	1948
#256	Hututu figure	7.13	—
#257	Saiyatasha (Long Horn) figure	7	1933
#286	Long Hair Kachina Bust pin	3.63	1948
#378	Two Horned Kkachina bust pin	3.13	1948
#379	Saiyatasha bust pin	2.63	—
#471	Hopi Snake Dancer bolo	4.63	1945
#497	Helelee figure	9.13	1944
#498	Zuni Dancer figure	8	1948
#711	Shalako pin	2.5	1958
#1009	Gleasy boys	6.25	1945
#1011	Rain Dancer figure	8	1946
#1012	Bear Clan figure	7.5	1946
#1034	Hopi Maiden pin	3	1942

Lambert Homer Jr.

No.	Figure	Ht.	Date
#191	Water Serpent pin/pendant	3.5	1942
#665	Mask pin	2.13	1934
#801	Salako disc pin/pendant	2.5	1955
#874	Sun Dancer figure	4.75	1949
#924	Shalako disc pin/pendant	2.25	1955

Jose Bowannie

No.	Figure	Ht.	Date
#194	Snake Dancer figure	4.25	1938
#348	Fire God figure	4.75	1965

Ted Edaakie

No.	Figure	Ht.	Date
#285	Eagle Dancer	3.63	1942
#456	Zuni Eagle Dance painting	14	1945

Charles Chuyate

No.	Figure	Ht.	Date
#460	Baffalo Dancer on canvas	16.5	—

Walter Nahktewa

No.	Figure	Ht.	Date
#143	Shalako pin	2	—
#162	Masks and Dancing figure rings	—	—
#394	two Shalako figures	1.75-3	1951
#442	Butterfly maiden bust pin	2.875	1929
#483	Fire God figure	2.125	1951
#725	Fire God pin	2.625	1950
#838	Hopi Snake Dancer pin	2.125	1929
#853	Prayer Plume tie clip	2.75	—
#936	Fire God figure	4.625	1951
#940	Yamuhakto (log carrier) pendant	2.25	—
#1003	Standing figure pin	2.5	1948

Teddy Weahkee

No.	Figure	Ht.	Date
#528	Koloowisi (water serpent) pin	3	1942
#551	Hututu bust pin/pendant	3.75	1930
#872	Mud Head painting on buckskin	58	1929
#873	Fire God painting on buckskin	64	1942
#1010	Mud Head carrying another kachina	5.75	1941

Red Leekela

No.	Figure	Ht.	Date
#287	Tablita Dancer	3.375	1945
#411	six Salimopia figures	6.5-7	1941
#779	Hopi Snake Dancer	3.75	1941
#876	Long Hair Kachina figure	4.875	1942

Bruce Zunie

No.	Figure	Ht.	Date
#23	Side Horn Dancer	7.75	1945
#496	Kachina figure	8.125	—

Jerry Watson

No.	Figure	Ht.	Date
#225	Shalako and Mud Head figures	2.5	1938
#402	Fire God figure	2.125	1935

Sam Poblano

No.	Figure	Ht.	Date
#347	Hopi Maiden Glinding Corn figure	4.75	1936

Daisy Poblano

No.	Figure	Ht.	Date
#762	Dancer figure	4.5	1943

Unknown Artist

No.	Figure	Ht.	Date
#637	Saiyatasha bust pin	3.5	—

Eleven pieces were made by Walter Nahktewa including Shalako, Fire God, Hopi Snake Dancer, and Yamuhakto.

Lambert Homer, Sr., further contributed five pieces, including Water Serpent, Shalako and Sun Dancer.

Teddy Weahkee provided three pieces, including Water Serpent, Hututu, and Mud Head Carrying Another Kachina, excluding two Kachina paintings on deer hide.

Red Leekela made four pieces, including Salimopia, Hopi Snake Dancer and Long Hair Kachina.

Bruce Zunie, Jose Bowannie, Ted Edaakie and Jerry Watson made two pieces each, and Sam Poblano, Charles Chuyate, Daisy Poblano and an unidentified artist made one piece each.

In total, twelve (or thirteen) Zuni artists made 53 Kachina jewelry pieces sold at the Sotheby Park Bernet's C. G. Wallace auction.

On the Taboo of Making Kachina Jewelry to Sell

When I visited a Zuni house, I noticed an altar hanging down from the ceiling of the main room. The altar consisted of Sun and Moon Kachinas and prayer sticks. These Kachina figures are for religious blessing of the house and the family. They were created by Bradley Edaakie, a son of Tony and Rita Edaakie. This kind of Bradley Edaakie's work is not for sale but is solely for religious use. I observed another altar created by him that consists of a Shalako figure and another Kachina. This Shalako Kachina is made of wood and fabrics. Bradley's father, Tony, also created this kind of religious work. I observed his wooden Knifewing figures as well at the same house with the Sun and Moon Kachina altar.

The owner of a gallery in Santa Fe told me these kind of Kachina figures made of wood, fabrics, and other materials had been recently negatively sanctioned againstsale. If a Kachina figure is made solely of wood in the way of Hopi Kachina carving, it can be sold without receiving this negative sanction. Consequently, older Zuni Kachina dolls made of wood, fabrics, and other materials at the gallery were set on the top of the shelf and not for sale, while those made of all wood were exhibited for sale.

As we see in my second book, *Sun Face and Hopi Bird in Zuni Jewelry*, there are many artists who make Sun Face figures. However, few artists make Sun Kachinas. I own only two pieces. I presume there may be a strong negative sanction against making Kachina figures in mosaic jewelry as well as in Kachina doll carving. I have heard it said several times that women, especially, should not make Kachina jewelry.

In order to avoid violating this kind of taboo, some approaches have been taken.

One is to create Kachinas of a different Pueblo. For example, Apache Mountain Spirit Dancer figures have been made by various Zuni artists. The famous Hopi Snake Dancers by Leo Poblano, John Lucio, and Edward Beyuka fall into this category as well.

The second approach is to make the figure differently from its authentic stature. In other words, the figure is deliberately designed incorrectly. As long as Kachinas in jewelry are not made correctly as religious figures, they may not violate the taboo. As only four or five colors of stones and shells can be used in jewelry, jewelry cannot be made to be identical to true religious figures. Nonetheless, there are not many artists who dare to make Kachina jewelry.

The third way is to make a Kachina figure featuring mixed characteristics of various Kachinas. With this approach, an artist may use only one characteristic from each modeled Kachina and mix the selected characteristics so that the end product does not look like any specific Kachina from the religious ceremony. This is a tactic which a Hopi Kachina doll carver, Tawaquaptewa, adopts. Barry Walsh (1998, p. 56) recollects: "Nonetheless, the katsina dolls that Tawaquaptewa sold to the public were unique. What distinguishes his dolls from all others of the same era (1920-1960) is that his carvings, ostensibly representing specific Katsinas, bear little resemblance to the actual Katsina figures that dance in the villages during the Hopi six-month ceremonial cycle. Thus, one cannot make a positive identification as to what Katsinas Tawaquaptewa's dolls are intended to represent."

I.
Anna Rita, Lambert Homer, Jr., and Zuni Mosaic Artists in this Book

Anna Rita and Lambert Homer, Jr.

Lambert Homer, Jr. (1937-1988) was once a lapidary for Preston Monongye. He and his wife, Anna Rita Huskie Homer, are not silversmiths, but lapidaries. Their designs are Knifewing, Rainbow Man, Buffalo Dancer, and Apache Gahn Dancer, which are inlaid in mother-of-pearl background or on a naturally shaped shell. These unset inlaid shell medallions are called "inserts."

One day in September, 2010, I visited Anna Rita Homer for the first time and asked about their work. She showed me two small unset Apache Mountain Spirit Dancer inserts, and I successfully purchased them. They sold their unset pieces to some traders who let Navajo or Zuni silversmiths set in the silver. Consequently, many of these final pieces sometimes resemble Navajo pieces in their silver work.

Lambert Homer, Jr., passed on in 1988 at age 51. If he had survived his heart attack, we would now have contemporary works by this couple to appreciate. We miss this great artist. As he was in charge of sawing out a design in a shell plate for his wife, she has not done lapidary work since his premature death in 1988. Therefore, my Apache Mountain Spirit Dancer inserts were inlaid before 1988.

Several days later, Anna Rita Homer sold an inlaid Rainbow Man pin to me. Now, we can clearly identify their works. The Knifewing and Rainbow Man pieces, which I attributed to Ida Poblano in my first book,

Knifewing Rainbow Man in Zuni Jewelry, seem to be misattributed and were likely made by Anna Rita and Lambert Homer, Jr., before 1988.

This Rainbow Man pin was made by Anna Rita and Lambert in the mosaic inlay in mother-of-pearl style in the 1980s. As it has two silver loops on its back, it might be a Manta pin as well. The insert is fastened with silver bezels and eight silver wires in place and is encircled by eight turquoise cabochons and silver wires. It measures 2.34 inches tall and consists of blue turquoise, red coral, white mother-of-pearl and black jet.

Mosaic inlay Rainbow Man in mother of pearl pin, Anna Rita and Lambert Homer Jr., no hallmark, 1980s, 1.84" x 2.34", $300-450.

A Rainbow Man ring with an insert made by Anna Rita and Lambert Homer, Jr., in the mosaic inlay in mother-of-pearl style. The silver work was done by Fred and Elsie Laconsello in the 1970s-1980s. When I saw the ring, I noticed its silver work was almost identical with that of the Knifewing ring featured in *Zuni Jewelry* (Bassman, 1992, p. 16), so I asked my son to send questions to the seller about its lapidary and silversmiths. In reply, the seller and long time trader, Ms. Vicky Kohnke, sent him back a detailed email. She taught him that there were four rings with the inserts being made by them: one Buffalo Dancer ring in the first row and two Mountain Spirit Dancer rings and one Knifewing ring in the last row. Through this transaction, I recognized Anna Rita's name for the first time. It measures 1.31 inches tall and consists of blue turquoise, red coral, white mother-of-pearl, and black jet.

Mosaic inlay Rainbow Man in mother of pearl ring, Anna Rita and Lambert Homer Jr. for the insert and Fred and Elsie Laconsello for the silverwork, Fred and Elsie Zuni, N. M., 1970s-1980s, 1.05" x 1.31", $120-180.

This Rainbow Man bolo with the insert was made by Anna Rita and Lambert Homer, Jr., or Lambert Homer, Sr., in the mosaic inlay in mother-of-pearl style in the 1950s-1960s. Although Anna Rita Homer confirmed it was their work, it may have been made by their father, based on the material used and the black incised lines on the feathers on his back. The insert measures 2.30 inches tall and consists of blue turquoise, red abalone, white mother-of-pearl, and black jet. The silver frame looks like a buckle shape and reminds me of Dan or Mike Simplicio's work.

Mosaic inlay Rainbow Man in clam shell bolo, Anna Rita and Lambert Homer Jr. or Lambert Homer Sr., no hallmark, 1950s-1960s, 2.60" x 3.03", $1200-1800.

This is a Knifewing bracelet with the insert made by Anna Rita and Lambert Homer, Jr., in the mosaic inlay in mother-of-pearl style in the 1970s-1980s. Its silver work may be done by a Navajo silversmith because of the excessiveness of silver work. The insert measures 1.97 inches tall and consists of blue turquoise, red coral, white mother-of-pearl, and black jet.

Mosaic inlay Knifewing in mother of pearl bracelet, Anna Rita and Lambert Homer Jr., no hallmark, 1970s-1980s, 1.74" x 2.21", $500-750.

Edward and Madeline Beyuka

Edward Beyuka (1921-2002) made his jewelry in 1956 for the first time. *Zuni: A Village of Silversmiths* (James Ostler et al., 1996, pp. 90-91) describes his learning process as follows:

> Although he had watched his parents making jewelry while he was growing up, he didn't make any himself until 1956. He practiced in the evening while his family was at the Night Dances. Then he taught his wife Madeline to work with him—she did the inlay and he did the silverwork.

Since their divorce, Edward has done both silver and lapidary works. I met him on December 24, 2001. When I told Faye Quandelacy that I would like to collect some Zuni mosaic jewelry, she took me to one of his sons at his trailer house. Edward's son was doing inlay work of a Buffalo Dancer for his father. I told him I would buy this Buffalo Dancer and further ordered from him a Little Fire God made by his father. While I relaxed in a room of the Inn at Halona, Edward Beyuka visited me without notice and asked me if I really wanted those two Kachina figures. I replied, "Yes, of course." Therefore, he made me a silver backing for the Little Fire God and two pairs of silver drums for bolo tips.

I visited Madeline Beyuka on December 28, 2009, and showed her my collection of their pieces. She showed me Edward's portrait which was taken for *Zuni: A Village of Silversmiths*. Madeline is a daughter of Simon Bica, a fetish carver. She showed me where her sister, Angela Cellicion, lived. Quanita Kallestewa, a potter, is also her sister.

Sybil Cachini

Sybil Cachini (1945-) is a younger sister of Robert Cachini, Sr., who taught her silver and lapidary work. She has inherited his designs and has made wonderful Kachina jewelry. Betty Natachu is their oldest sister. I first met Sybil on January 8, 2011, and acquired her Ram Kachina pendant and bolo. I asked her about Robert Cachini, Sr., and how to identify his jewelry. She confirmed several pieces of jewelry were his, including the Antelope Kachina pin, which was previously attributed as hers by Bassman (2006, p. 29). She is in her mid-60s now.

She made a Ram Kachina bolo for the governor and Antelope Kachina bolo for the lieutenant governor of Zia Pueblo in 2006.

Robert Cachini, Sr.

Robert Cachini, Sr., (1939-2002) often put his hallmark, "R. C. Sr.," on his pieces. His Antelope Kachina ring appears in the book by Wright (2000). His designs are Antelope Kachina, Ram Kachina, and Wohtemthla (cannot be accurately translated in English).

Dexter Cellicion

After Dexter Cellicion (1931-1999) lost his first wife, Rosemary, he married Mary Ann and made various Kachina jewelry during the 1950s and 1960s. After she passed on, he married Eva. We can see their Sun Face pins made in the mosaic inlay style in the 1980s in *Zuni Jewelry* (Bassman, 2006, p. 29). They are colorful Sun Face pieces.

Some of my informants attributed many older mosaic inlay pieces to Oliver Cellicion and Dexter Cellicion. Considering it, Dexter Cellicion should be one of the master artists in the Zuni jewelry history although his work has been featured only in one book (Bassman, 2006, pp. 29 and 34). I met Eva Cellicion in December 2009 and interviewed for a short time at the doorway of her house. She seemed to know little about his older pieces from the 1940s to 1960s.

Andrew Dewa

Andrew Dewa was taken care by Anthony and Rita Edaakie because of his lack of a caregiver. Later, Anthony gave him a pattern of his Antelope Kachina after which Andrew created his own Antelope Kachina design. He made other Kachinas into jewelry including Sun Kachina, Shalako and so on. Don Dewa is his younger brother.

Theodore and Margaret Edaakie

Theodore Edaakie (1911-1987) is the third oldest of the Edaakie brothers. Although his name did not appear in the Adair's list, his Eagle Dancer, owl, and road runner pins were included in the *The C. G. Wallace Collection of American Indian Art* auction catalog. After he passed on, Margaret sold her lapidary works, which were mounted on silver backings by Leonard Martza, to the Pueblo Trading Post. Although a book describes Dennis Edaakie and Theodore Edaakie as brothers, Theodore is neither a son of Merle Edaakie nor a brother of Dennis Edaakie.

Anthony and Rita Edaakie

Tony Edaakie (1927-1989) is the youngest of the Edaakie brothers. He is a jeweler as well as a painter and a wood carver of Kachina figures, including Knifewing, Sun Kachina, and Moon Kachina. They put their hallmark, "Tony + Rita," on their pieces. Their son, Bradley, has made wood carvings for the Zunis. Another son, Raylan, has made wonderful contemporary mosaic jewelry.

Tony and Rita raised Andrew Dewa because he lacked a caregiver in his childhood, and they gave him a pattern of their Antelope Kachina design after which his earlier Antelope Kachina pieces were made. Therefore, their art tradition is transmitted not only by their sons, Bradley and Raylan, but also by Andrew Dewa.

Lambert Homer, Sr.

Lambert Homer, Sr., (1917-1972) is no doubt one of the greatest mosaic overlay and channel inlay artists in the Zuni jewelry history. His works have been continuously featured in many books, including the famous *The C. G. Wallace Collection of American Indian Art* auction catalog (1975). This catalogue features numerous incredible works by Lambert Homer, Sr., although they are all attributed to Lambert Homer, Jr., including a historic turquoise-inlaid belt made in collaboration with Roger Skeet. In many cases, the name Lambert Homer, Jr., might actually mean Lambert Homer, Sr.

His wife, Juanita Othole Homer, is a sister of Mary Kallestewa.

Mary Kallestewa

Mary Kallestewa (1915-1987) is one of the artists representing the famous C. G. Wallace collection. Mary is a sister of Lambert Homer, Sr.'s wife, Juanita Othole Homer. She worked at the trading post with her husband, Lapelle (Slaney, 1998, 31).

She taught Angela Cellicion how to do silversmithing and lapidary work. She ran a burger shop named Mary's Corner. She was a wonderful dancer who danced in the muscular manner. Lapelle passed on in March, 2011.

Curtis Kucate

Curtis Kucate (1936-) is a son of Theodore and Susie Kucate and a younger brother of Thelma Sheche. He learned silversmithing by watching the work of Jerry Dixon, his mother's brother. Jerry Dixon is one of the representative artists of the C. G. Wallace Trading Post who works in the cluster work style. According to Curtis, he got a lot of orders through Tobe Turpen. Curtis Kucate mainly works in the channel inlay style; however, on a rare occasion, he utilizes the nugget style as well.

Morris "Red" Leekela

Red Leekela used to make Kachina jewelry for C. G. Wallace, when he was very young. However, his close relatives persuaded him not to make it any more, and he switched from Kachina jewelry to ordinary designs such as Knifewing, Rainbow Man, Sun Face, and so on. He lived until his mid-80s and passed on in the mid-2000s. Marietta Soceah is his sister.

His nickname "Red" is based on his beautiful red hair. His first name was Morris, and he had a husky voice.

Leonard Lonjose

Leonard Lonjose (1934-2004) is a step-son of Mabel Lonjose and once was married to Edith Tsabetsaye. His designs are Apache Mountain Spirit Dancer and Quail Bird with a lot of silver work that looks unusual for the Zuni jewelry.

Mabel Lonjose

Mabel Lonjose (1914-2001) is the step-mother of Leonard Lonjose. Her signature piece includes a gigantic olla maiden figure. Her hallmark is in the book, *Hallmarks in the Southwest* (Wright, 1989, p. 109).

John Lucio

John Lucio (1919-1984) is very famous for his Eagle Dancer design. *Zuni: the Art and the People* (Bell, 1975, p. 20) says that he has been making jewelry since 1950, while *American Indian Jewelry I* (Schaaf, 2003, p. 228) notes that he was already active in the 1930s, based on the *The C. G. Wallace Collection of American Indian Art* auction catalog (Sotheby Park Bernet, 1975). According to the former book, he once was a member of highly esteemed Zuni firefighters; therefore, he might have been a part-time jeweler before 1950. He made a variety of wonderful Kachina jewelry, including Hopi Snake Dancer, Buffalo Dancer and Hoop Dancer, other than his famous Eagle Dancer.

Vera Luna

Vera Luna (1930-1982) is a daughter of Bell Luna. She had made a variety of Kachina Jewelry including Apache Mountain Spirit Dancer.

Leonard Martza

Leonard Martza is one of the artists who represents the famous C. G. Wallace collection. He is one of the oldest artists still active today. He used to work for C. G. Wallace's Trading Post, and his service started in the 1950s. He has also worked for the Pueblo Trading in Zuni Pueblo since then. When I visited Zuni in the summer of 2003, he was providing silver work for pins and bracelets for mosaic overlay artists such as Margaret Edaakie and Betty Natachu.

Walter Nahktewa

Even though little is known about Walter Nahktewa (- early1960s), some information is available. He is one of the representative artists of C. G. Wallace collection. His 11 pieces were auctioned at the famous C. G. Wallace collection auction. The oldest pieces among them were made in 1929, while half of them were made from the late 1940s to the early 1950s. Therefore, he can be considered as an outstanding artist even when compared with other greats of his time, such as Leo Poblano, Lambert Homer, Sr., and Frank Vacit.

Tony Ohmsatte

Tony Ohmsatte works in the mosaic inlay in mother-of-pearl style and is famous for his Apache Mountain Spirit Dancer design. This design is almost identical to the one made by Leonard Lonjose. However, there is one point in which we can distinguish Tony's design from Leonard's. While the former has a flat line between the headdress and head, the latter has a curvilinear one.

Quincy Peynetsa

Little was known about Quincy Peynetsa (1943-1982) except that he used to make some wonderful Kachina jewelry in the silver overlay/mosaic inlay style. One of my collector friends in Texas sent me a photo of Shalako bolo and mentioned his name as the probable artist. It reminded me of the work of Frank Vacit, but one of Frank's daughters denied it was her father's work. I have searched for Quincy's name among various reference books. However, I could not find any information about him. A gallery homepage mentioned his name as a probable artist based on the hallmarks, QDP.

Except for a few middle-aged artists, most older Zuni artists do not know his name. Some said his name should be Quintus Peynetsa or Quincy Panteah. Nevertheless, he surely existed and made marvelous mosaic jewelry in the silver overlay/mosaic inlay style.

Quincy Peynetsa had a tragically premature death in 1982. He signed his signature on some of his pieces, but many pieces remained unsigned. He made Kachina jewelry including Mudhead and Shalako, resembling the ones Frank Vacit made. Quincy's skills are outstanding. Unfortunately, he died before developing his own style of art and achieving artistic virtuosity.

Augustine and Rosalie Pinto

Augustine Pinto (1921-2002) and his wife Rosalie are most famous for their raised mosaic Kachina jewelry such as Mud Head, Koshare Clown and Shalako. Their gigantic Shalako bolo may be one of the most gorgeous pieces ever made in Zuni jewelry history. In comparison, his Knifewing and Rainbow man designs have been little known.

Ida Vacit Poblano

Ida Vacit (1925-1987) married Leo Poblano in 1947, and they used to live where their daughter, Veronica Poblano, founded her own gallery: Galleria Poblano.

After Leo's tragic death during fire-fighting in California, Ida Vacit Poblano completed many of her husband's unfinished pieces (Slaney, 1998, p. 28). As she was not a silversmith but a lapidary, she sold her mosaic pieces without silver backings to galleries such as C. G. Wallace, John Kennedy, Tobe Turpen, and others (Harmsen, Ed., 1988, p. 4). Since silver works of her mosaic overlay pieces were sometimes done by Navajo silversmiths, including Ike Wilson and Mary Morgan, these finished pieces inevitably exhibited a Navajo taste. As to her mosaic lapidary work, all of her pieces have an authentic Zuni feel. She is most famous for Zuni Kachina figures from the Harmsen Collection, which are joint works with Navajo silversmith, Mary Morgan.

Leo Poblano

Leo Poblano (1905-1959) is one of the greatest artists in Zuni jewelry history without doubt. He is a nephew of Teddy Weahkee. He married Daisy Hooee Nampeyo, a Hopi/Tewa potter and a grand-daughter of the single most famous potter, Nampeyo, in 1939. He taught her Zuni lapidary work, and she taught him three dimensional relief techniques, which she had learned at L'Ecole des Beau Arts in Paris in 1929 (C. Slaney, 1998, p. 28). They divorced in the early 1940s. One of the contemporary representative mosaic lapidaries, Shirley Benn, is the daughter from her earlier marriage.

Leo Poblano then married Ida Vacit in 1947. They had four children, including Veronica Poblano, Charlotte Eustace, and Faye Lonjose, all of whom are marvelous jewelers. He died tragically in 1959 while fire-fighting in California.

He did not convert to an electric grinder until the late 1950s (Slaney, 1998, p. 28) although it was introduced to Zuni in 1954. The face of his ceremonial dancers and Kachinas are carved in the relief techniques without black pigment. It should be his signature.

Elliott Qualo

Elliott Qualo (1930-1974) was included in the Arizona Highways Hall of Fame of artists (*Arizona Highways*, August 1974, pp. 32 and 44) even though he was relatively young and a contemporary of Veronica Poblano, Ed Beyuka, Porfilio Sheyka, Dennis Edaakie, and Lee and Mary Weebothee. *Arizona Highways Magazine* featured his Apache Mountain Spirit Dancer set for men and a Ram's Head pin. He was recognized as one of the master artists by the 1970s.

Ralph Quam

His name appears in *Zuni Jewelry* (Bassman, 1992, p. 12), where Shalako and Zuni altar pins are attributed to him. His Shalako pin is almost identical with the one made by Leo Poblano. Those two pins were circa 1940s, so he was active during the era when Kachina jewelry began to be made in quantity.

Dixon and Martha Hustito Shebola

Martha Hustito Shebola is one of Alonzo Hustito's daughters, along with Linda Hustito Wheeler and Erma Hustito. She married Dixon Shebola (1937-1976), a son of Jesephine Nahohai. They made wonderful mosaic jewelry and toured around to attend art shows. They were very successful and popular in the 1970s. During their absence, my friend, Milford Nahohai, did baby-sitting for their children.

Their signature piece was a Plains Indian Warrior with a war bonnet in the mosaic inlay style. This one is presented in the book: *Sky Stone and Silver* (Rosnek and Stacey, 1976, pp. 102-103). However, this signature piece was copied outside the United States so well that we must be careful to purchase it on the antique market. If a flower-like ornament on the Warrior's right hand is removable and usable as a tie tack, it should be their authentic piece. I also noticed that Dixon signed his signature as Shebala, using an electric pen.

Porfilio and Ann Sheyka

Porfilio and Ann Sheyka had made a variety of birds including quail, owl, and eagle, as well as rabbit and frog. They used to make an Eagle Kachina, as well, since it appeared in the *Arizona Highways* Hall of Fame Classic and in the book by Ray Manlay (1975, p. 24).

Myra and Lee Tucson

Myra Tucson is an accomplished jeweler who represents Zuni artists in the 1960s. In 1965, she attended the "Southwest Indian Arts II," held at California Palace of the Legion of Honor in San Francisco, to show her art, along with an innovative Navajo artist, Kenneth Begay (Schaaf, 2003, p. 314).

Since many pieces are attributed to her by my informants, she is recognized as one of the representative artists by surviving older artists.

Frank Vacit

Frank Vacit (1915-1999) is one of the representative artists of the famous C. G. Wallace Collection. He married one of Leekya Deyuse's daughters, Elizabeth Leekya (1919-2005). Elizabeth was a lapidary as well as a bead work artist. His younger brother, Homer Vacit, is a wonderful mosaic jewelry artist as well. Frank has a son, Gary Vacit, and three daughters, including Bessie and Jovanna. They are all skilled lapidaries. One book (Schaaf, 2003, p. 257) introduces Leo Poblano's last wife, Ida Vacit Poblano, as a niece of Frank Vacit while another book (Deborah C. Slaney, 1998, p. 42) introduces her as Frank's daughter.

One of Frank's daughters told me that his friend in California presented Frank with a gigantic sea turtle shell in the 1950s, and Frank used it as a back-ground for mosaic figures instead of overlaid silver one.

Joe Zunie

Joe Zunie is from the Zunie family, including brothers William and Lincoln, and their father Willie. Joe made wonderful ceremonial dancers, domestic animals including horses and cows, and even carp. He added etching on his pieces, which makes them realistic.

Lincoln and Helen Zunie

Lincoln Zunie is still active, although his wife, Helen Zunie, has passed on. He has made Eagle Dancer, covered wagon, ox, and horse. I got a covered wagon bolo directly from him in June, 2010.

William Zunie

William Zunie (1938-1983) was another of the Zunie brothers who used to make Eagle dancer and Sun Face. He is the father of Patty Zunie Edaakie, who is the wife of Raylan Edaakie.

II.
Kachinas and Ceremonial Dancers

Classification of Kachinas and Ceremonial Dancers

I used to try classifying Kachinas and Ceremonial Dancers in Zuni jewelry by myself, but I experienced much difficulty. Therefore, I asked my Zuni friends for tips on classification. They showed me the difference between Kachinas and Social Dancers. For example, if a figure wears full-feathered bonnet and is painted with red pigment around his eyes and cheeks, this figure should be a Comanche Kachina. If the figure lacks such paint in its face, it should be a Social Dancer of Comanche Indian. They showed me some ways to classify Kachinas into Corn Dancers and Rain Dancers in addition to Shalako-related Kachinas. In this chapter, I will first describe Shalako-related Kachinas. Next, I introduce Corn Dancers in Winter, Rain Dancers in Summer, and Social Dancers. Finally, I discuss the characteristics of Kachinas and Ceremonial Dancers from other Pueblos or tribes.

Kachinas in Shalako Ceremony

The Shalako Ceremony is one of the most gorgeous Zuni religious ceremonies, and, for the most part, it has been open to the public. Even if one is from other pueblos or tribes or is a non-native American, one can observe this ceremony. As far as one respects the ceremony and follows the rules and regulations for tourists observing the Zuni religious ceremonies, one's visit is permitted.

Kachinas in the Shalako ceremony consist of six Shalakos and their alternates, one Long Horn Kachina or Saiyatasha, one Hututu, two Yamhakto or Log Carrier Kachinas, two Salimopia or Warrior Kachinas (all six Salimopia appear in three years), one Shulawitsi or Little Fire God and his ceremonial father, and ten Koyemshi or Mud Head Kachinas.

Ida Vacit Poblano once made a few sets of these Kachinas. They are included in the Harmsen Collection and the Kennedy Collection. The latter set is currently housed in the Kennedy Museum of Art at Ohio University.

I saw another set at the Tobe Turpen's Trading Post in around 2000 (the present Perry Null Trading Company). Leonard Martza made a similar set, which consists of seven Shalako Kachina figures and additional three Rain Dancers or Long Hair Kachinas, and this set won a blue ribbon in the 1960s. He gave me a photo of the set in 2009.

A choker necklace of five Kachinas in the Shalako ceremony and two Sun Faces was made by Leonard Martza on April 10, 2011. When I visited him at his home on April 5, 2011, he showed me the drawing of the necklace and half-done pieces of silver parts and unpolished figures. All four figures were almost finished, except for Salimopia (also known as the Warrior Kachina); its head was completed but it lacked the upper body. Two Sun Faces were not present either. As soon as I saw the piece, I asked him to finish the choker by the last day of my Zuni stay. The center is a full figure of the Shalako Kachina which measures 1.4 inches tall.

To his right is the Saiyatasha or Long Horn Kachina, and to the left is Hututu or the Deputy of Saiyatasha. They measure 1.33 inches tall. The next to Siyatasha is Yamuhakto (Log Carrier Kachina), and the next to Hututu is Salimopia (Warrior Kachina). They are an inch tall. The most difficult part of its construction seems to be making hand-made coils of silver wire that connect silver platelets together.

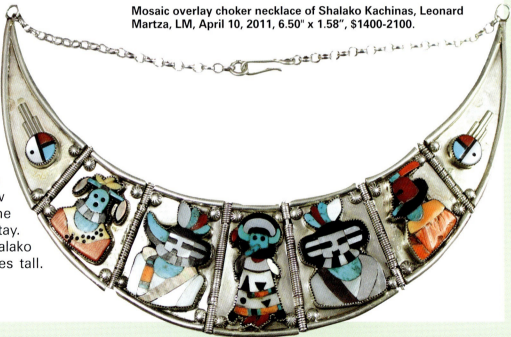

Mosaic overlay choker necklace of Shalako Kachinas, Leonard Martza, LM, April 10, 2011, 6.50" x 1.58", $1400-2100.

Shalako

Shalako is the courier or messenger of Rain God, which stands 10 feet tall. Six Shalako Kachinas appear in the Shalako ceremony. The first Shalako figure in Zuni Jewelry might have been made by Jerry Watson in 1938, followed by Leo Poblano in 1939, and later by Lambert Homer, Sr., and Walter Nahktewa in the 1950s.

This Shalako bolo was made by Myra Tucson in the mosaic inlay style in the late 1960s. It has a third prize ribbon from the 1971 Intertribal Indian Ceremonials, and Myra's hallmark of a bird's foot or track is located on the back. The bolo has two matching tips of eagle feathers. The beak, black collar, and skin-colored fur around the shoulder stick out from the surface of the figure, which enhances the figure's three-dimensional effect. The figure measures 5 inches tall and consists of blue turquoise, red coral, white mother-of-pearl, black jet, and yellow shell.

Mosaic inlay Shalako bolo, Myra Tucson, bird's foot or track, 1960s, 2" x 5", $1200-1800.

Myra Tucson's hallmark

A Shalako bolo made by Myra Tucson in the mosaic inlay style in the 1940s-1950s is based on the two W-shaped handmade wire clasps. The beak and collar stick out from the surface as well. It measures 3.2 inches tall and consists of blue turquoise, pink/red abalone, white mother-of-pearl, black jet, and unidentified stone or shell for the fur around the shoulder. As both of them are good examples of older Zuni Kachina jewelry, we can safely say that Myra Tucson is one of the master Zuni jewelers.

Mosaic inlay Shalako bolo, Myra Tucson, bird's foot or track, 1960s, 2" x 5", $1200-1800.

Frank Vacit made this Shalako bolo in the silver overlay and mosaic inlay style in the 1950s-1960s, based on the "Bennett Pat. Pend. C31" inscriptions on the back. Although his "ear of corn" hallmark or signature are not on the back, stamps on the borders clearly show it is his work. One of his daughters told me that she owned the stamp. The black collar sticks out from the surface and gives this bolo a slight three-dimensional effect. The bolo measures 2.3 inches tall and the Shalako figure measures 1.85 inches tall. Considering this size, his extreme intricacy in the lapidary and the silver work are evident. It consists of blue turquoise, red coral, white mother-of-pearl, black jet, and iridescent abalone.

Silver overlay and mosaic inlay Shalako bolo, Frank Vacit, no hallmark, 1950s-1960s, 2" x 2.3", $1200-1800.

This flush mosaic inlay Shalako bust pendant was made by an unknown Zuni artist in the 1950s-1960s. Although it has been attributed to Dexter Cellicion by one of my informants, I am not sure about this attribution. It has a black rectangular head. It measures 1.5 inches tall and consists of blue/green turquoise, red coral, white mother-of-pearl, black jet, and brown tortoise shell.

Mosaic inlay Shalako head pin, unknown artist, no hallmark, 1950s-1960s, 1.3" x 1.5", $100-150.

Edward Beyuka made this Shalako bolo in the mosaic inlay style from the 1980s-1990s. This estimation of the date is based on the fact that there is no inscription on the moving part of the Bennett bolo clasps, while its shape is as same as the ones being sold between 1967-1983. Some of the stones/shells are set a little higher from the surface; some of them are curved. The bolo measures 4.88 inches tall and consists of blue turquoise, red coral, yellow lip oyster shell, white mother-of-pearl, black jet, and iridescent abalone shell.

Mosaic inlay Shalako bolo, Edward Beyuka, EAB ZUNI, 1980s-1990s, 1.60" x 4.88", $1000-1500.

This Shalako bolo was made by Andrew Dewa in the mosaic overlay style in the 1980s-1990s. His pieces are always made in the three-dimensional mosaic overlay style, which is observable in the larger piece made by Merle Edaakie (Sei, 2010, 70). The face and horn are set above the surface, and two black vertical parts are set below the surface. This is an extremely difficult and demanding mosaic technique. Moreover, his Shalako design has no similarity to those made by any other artists in Zuni jewelry history and is successful.

His piece seems technically and artistically perfect and showcases his own unique design. He is surely a true artist. It measures 4.125 inches tall and consists of blue turquoise, red coral, gold lip oyster shell, white mother-of-pearl, black jet, and iridescent abalone shell.

Mosaic overlay Shalako bolo, Andrew Dewa, A. DEWA ZUNI, 1980s-1990s, 1.875" x 4.125", $1000-1500.

A Shalako bracelet made by Rosalie and Augustine Pinto in mosaic inlay in the tortoise shell style in the 1950s-1960s. Although their ARP hallmark is not found, the silver work should be theirs. The face and body are straight forward while the feet point to his left. The total Shalako figure measures just less than 2 inches. Considering this smaller size, their intricate mosaic work is incredible. They once made a gorgeous gigantic Shalako bolo (Ostler et al., 1996, p. 127).

Mosaic inlay in tortoise shell Shalako bolo, Rosalie and Augustine Pinto, no hallmark, 1950s-1960s, 1.5" x 2" for the insert, $800-1200.

A Shalako bolo made by Quincy Peynetsa in silver overlay and mosaic inlay style in the 1960s-1970s. His style and design remind me of Frank Vacit's. However, one of Vacit's daughters denied that it was her father's and attributed it to Quincy Peynetsa. While Frank Vacit's pieces usually have a stamped border on the edge, Quincy's pieces do not have such a border. This bolo measures 2 inches tall and consists of blue turquoise, red coral, white mother-of-pearl, and black jet. His technical excellence is evident. However, this bolo did not seem to show that the artist had established the unique design of his own at the point of its making.

Silver overlay and mosaic inlay Shalako bolo, Quincy Peynetsa, no hallmark, 1970s-1980s, 1.57" x 2", $200-300.

Rosary Calavaza made this Shalako bolo in the mosaic overlay style in the 1970s-1980s. While the face, horns, and eagle feathers with incised lines are set flush, the carved black collar and green necklace are set slightly higher; the red-and-white beak sticks out much higher. This technique is a raised mosaic overlay technique that is very difficult to execute and still remains as a traditional Zuni lapidary method. It measures 2.32 inches tall and consists of green turquoise, red coral, white mother-of-pearl, and black jet.

Mosaic overlay Shalako bolo, Rosary Calavaza, Kokopelli figure sandwiched by C and R, 1970s-1980s, 1.50" x 2.32", $300-450.

Saiyatasha

Saiyatasha (Long Horn Kachina) is the leader of the Council of Gods (Saiyatasha party) which consists of Little Fire God, his ceremonial father, Hututu (The deputy of Saiyatasha), Yamuhakto (The Wood Carrier), and Salimopia (Warrior Kachina). Saiyatasha is the Rain Priest of the North and the most prestigious Kachina along with Pautiwa (Kachina Chief). Saiyatasha appears only at the Shalako ceremony.

A lot of Long Horn jewelry has been made by various artists. The most famous one may be the bust pin made by Leo Poblano (Sotheby Park Bernet, 1975, #379). Some parts of the pin are set a little bit higher, providing this Saiyatasha pin a three-dimensional effect.

Above is a Saiyatasha pin probably made by Leo Poblano in the mosaic overlay style in the 1940s-1950s. Some parts, including a black-and-white collar, are set slightly higher from the base, and three white feathers and one black one are carved so that they look like real feathers. Moreover, the statue is adorned with twelve petit-point turquoise cabochons. It measures 3.04 inches tall and consists of blue/green turquoise, red spiny oyster, white mother-of-pearl, and black jet.

At the right is a Saiyatasha bolo made by Dexter Cellicion in the mosaic inlay style in the 1940s-1950s, based on the W-shaped double wire bolo clasps. This attribution was made by three of my informants independently. Several years ago, one of my collector friends was extremely pleased to hear from an experienced trader that an almost identical Saiyatasha piece was Lambert Homer, Sr.'s piece. All stones and shells are set flush. A unique feature of this Saiyatasha figure is that the black forehead is split into two parts; feathers are set between them. It measures 1.77 inches across and consists of blue/green turquoise, red spiny oyster, white mother-of-pearl and black jet.

Mosaic overlay Saiyatasha pin, Leo Poblano, no hallmark, 1940s-1950s, 2.43"x 3.04", $2000-3000.

Mosaic inlay Saiyatasha bolo, Dexter Cellicion, no Hallmark, 1940s-1950s, 1.77" across, $1000-1500.

Dexter Cellicion's Saiyatasha bracelet could be a set with the bolo described just above. The forehead is split into two and three feathers are set between the halves. It was made by him in the mosaic inlay style in the 1940s-1950s. Two red parts are added under the collar, which might be his necklace, and two adornments, consisting of two eagle feathers and one from a parrot and a cloud symbol, are set on the both sides of the Saiyatasha figure. Stamped silver drops which look like flowers are unique to this silversmith. The figure measures 1.53 inches tall and consists of blue turquoise, red spiny oyster, white mother-of-pearl, and black jet.

Mosaic inlay Saiyatasha bracelet, Dexter Cellicion, no hallmark, 1940s-1950s, 1.85" x 1.53", $1000-1500.

Another Saiyatasha bracelet was made by Dexter Cellicion in the mosaic inlay style in the 1950s-1960s. Although it is similar with the bracelet described at the left, there are some different points between them. The forehead of this figure is not split and the ear looks rectangular instead of crescent-shaped and curvilinear. Nevertheless, the overall impression of this figure is very similar with the one described above. In addition, the adornments on the both sides of the figure are almost identical between the two. The side ornaments look like a combination of feathers and a cloud symbol. The figure measures 1.58 inches tall and consists of green turquoise, red spiny oyster, white mother-of-pearl, and black jet.

Mosaic inlay Saiyatasha bracelet, Dexter Cellicion, no hallmark, 1940s-1950s, 1.86" x 1.58", $1000-1500.

An unknown Zuni artist made this Saiyatasha pin in the 1940s-1960s in the mosaic overlay style. It is made all flush. The face and ear are rectangular and two white feathers are set vertically. These features give this pin a static impression. Meanwhile, the unique point of this pin seems to reside in the silver work under the figure. Three clusters of flower petals highlights this figure. The figure itself and the entire pin measure 1.69 and 2.33 inches respectively. The figure is inlaid with blue turquoise, red spiny oyster, white mother-of-pearl, and black jet.

Mosaic overlay Saiyatasha pin, artist unknown, no Hallmark, 1940s-1960s, 2.08" x 2.33", $300-450.

This Saiyatasha bolo in the mosaic inlay style was made by Edward Beyuka in the 1980s-1990s. It can also be set on the table because it has a clasp which accepts the pin of its stand. Some parts are set a little above the base, which gives this pin a three-dimensional effect. Some parts are carved as well. It measures 4.50 inches tall and consists of blue turquoise, red coral, yellow-lip mother-of-pearl, white mother-of-pearl, black jet, and a black-and-brown shell.

Mosaic inlay Saiyatasha bolo, Edward Beyuka, EAB, 1980s-1990s, 2.14" x 4.5", $1000-1500.

36

Edward Beyuka made this Saiyatasha bolo in the mosaic inlay style in the 1980s-1990s. I bought these two bolos at the same gallery in Gallup. The sticker on the back says it is from the 1970s or older. However, this second one should be made in the 1980s, and the first one seems to be made in the late 1980s or 1990s. This second piece is bigger than the first, measuring 5.22 inches tall. It consists of blue turquoise, red coral, yellow-lip mother-of-pearl, abalone shell, white mother-of-pearl, black jet, and black-and-brown shell. Both of them raise their right knees, which gives these figures a feeling of movement.

Mosaic inlay Saiyatasha bolo, Edward Beyuka, EAB, 1980s-1990s, 2.84" x 5.22", $1200-1800.

Andrew Dewa made this Saiyatasha bolo in the 1970s-1980s in the raised mosaic overlay style. This time frame is estimated due to the stamped upside-down inscriptions of "Bennett Pat. Pend." His right arm is set higher and the yellow sleeves are carved. This figure looks extremely realistic. It measures 4.55 inches tall and consists of blue turquoise, red coral, yellow-lip mother-of-pearl, white mother-of-pearl, and black jet. Andrew Dewa was surely one of the contemporary master artists. We miss him very much.

Mosaic overlay Saiyatasha bolo, Andrew Dewa, A. DEWA ZUNI, 1970s-1980s, 2.14" x 4.55", $1200-1800.

This Saiyatasha pin in the mosaic overlay style was probably made by Red Leekela in the 1940s-1950s. Some parts are set a little bit higher than the remaining ones. It is marked "-MK.LS," but this might be a price mark of a trading post. Dale Stuart King attributes a similar Saiyatasha pin to an Edaakie boy (King, 1976, p. 175), but none of the Zuni artists attribute it to an artist from the various Edaakie families. Finally, I decided to ask Mr. Perry Null of the Perry Null Trading Company. He considered its attribution for a while and suggested that the artist might be Red Leekela. As I described earlier, his four kachina jewelry pieces are featured in the *The C. G. Wallace Collection of American Indian Art* auction catalog. However, no piece in my collection had been attributed to him to that point; this is the first. It has a turquoise nugget adornment over the right shoulder of the figure. This is a unique characteristic of this artist's Saiyatasha design which is found in the following small Saiyatasha pendant and a small Hututu pendant made by this artist. The horn of the figure is not so long, although its English name is the Long Horn Kachina. The figure measures 2.09 inches tall and consists of blue/green turquoise, red spiny oyster, white mother-of-pearl, and black jet.

Mosaic overlay Saiyatasha pin, Red Leekela, -MK. LS, 1940s-1950s, 1.82" x 2.09", $1000-1500.

A Saiyatasha pendant made by Red Leekela in the mosaic overlay style in the 1940s-1950s. Some parts are set slightly higher than the others. It has a coral adornment on the right shoulder of the figure and a relatively short horn. It is only 1.10 inches tall. Considering this smaller size, this artist presents incredible lapidary skill. It consists of blue turquoise, red coral, white mother-of-pearl, and black jet.

Mosaic overlay Saiyatasha pendant, Red Leekela, no hallmark, 1940s-1950s, 0.99" x 1.10", $600-900.

This Saiyatasha ring made by Dexter Cellicion in the mosaic inlay style in the 1950s-1960s shares the same style as his Hututu, Shlawitsi, and Mud Head rings in this book. It measures 0.93 inches across and consists of blue turquoise, red coral, white mother-of-pearl, and black jet.

Mosaic inlay Saiyatasha ring, Dexter Cellicion, no hallmark, 1950s-1960s, 0.93" across, $150-225.

This Saiyatasha bolo made by Dexter Cellicion in the mosaic inlay style in the 1950s-1960s is not a flush mosaic inlay. The surfaces of parts have curvature and are set in the channel. The figure has a triangular mouth, which is characteristic of his pieces. The black-and-white collar is formed straight while almost all of the other Saiyatasha figures have curvilinear forms. This straight collar is unique to this bolo and the next piece. This piece measures 2.47 inches tall and consists of blue turquoise, red coral, white mother-of-pearl, and black jet.

Mosaic inlay Saiyatasha bolo, Dexter Cellicion, no hallmark, 1950s-1960s, 1.67" x 2.47", $300-450.

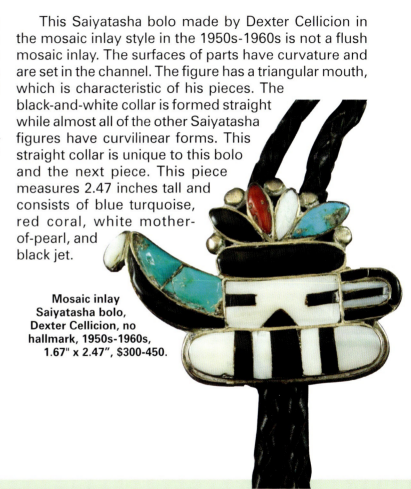

This Saiyatasha bolo was probably made by Dexter Cellicion in the mosaic inlay style between the late 1960s and the early 1980s. It is in the flush inlay style. There is a turquoise feather hung from the tip of the long horn. The figure has a turquoise necklace and a straight collar. It measures 1.50 inches tall and consists of blue turquoise, red coral, white mother-of-pearl, and black jet.

Mosaic inlay Saiyatasha bolo, Dexter Cellicion?, no hallmark, 1960s-1980s, 1.95" x 1.49", $200-300.

Vera Luna made this Saiyatasha bolo in the mosaic inlay style in the 1980s. Some parts are set a little higher than the remaining ones. Her colorful lapidary work is done with extreme precision, especially for the costume and moccasins. In addition, the matching Shalako face bolo tips enhance the attractiveness of the bolo. Although the face looks smaller compared with the legs, her lapidary skill is way above average. It measures 3.82 inches tall and consists of blue turquoise, red coral, iridescent abalone shell, white mother-of-pearl, and black jet.

Mosaic inlay Saiyatasha bolo, Vera Luna, V. L., 1980s, 1.97" x 3.82", $400-600.

Hututu

Hututu is the Rain Priest of the South and the deputy of Saiyatasha. Hututu, like Saiyatasha, appears only in the Shalako ceremony. He is named for his deep voiced call of "Hu-tu-tu!" (Wright, 1985, p. 34). Hututu has been made in jewelry much less than his chief, Saiyatasha. Compared with 14 pieces of Saiyatasha I own, I have collected only 2 Hututu pieces.

On this Hututu pendant, made by Red Leekela in the mosaic overlay style in the 1940s-1950s, the figure has a red coral nugget on his right shoulder for adornment. Some black and white parts are raised a little higher from the remaining ones. These characteristics are common between the two Saiyatasha and Hututu pendants made by him. It measures 1.41 inches tall and consists of blue turquoise, red coral, white mother-of-pearl, and black jet.

Mosaic overlay Hututu pendant, Red Leekela, no hallmark, 1940s-1950s, 0.97" x 1.41", $600-900.

This Hututu ring was made by Dexter Cellicion in the mosaic inlay style in the 1950s-1960s. It has a triangular mouth, which is characteristic of his pieces. An almost identical ring without the white mother-of-pearl background is featured in *Southwest Silver Jewelry* (Baxter, 2001, pp. 147 and 152) along with other Kachina rings and a bracelet in the Saiyatasha party. The ring base measures 0.98 inches across, and the figure measures 0.58 inches tall. Considering this smaller size, his lapidary skill is way beyond the average. It consists of blue turquoise, red coral, yellow-lip mother-of-pearl, white mother-of-pearl, and black jet.

Mosaic inlay Hututu ring, Dexter Cellicion, no hallmark, 1950s-1960s, 0.98" across, $150-225.

Yamuhakto

Yamuhakto, also known as Wood Carrier, is an assistant of Saiyatasha and Hututu. In Shalako ceremony, two Yamuhakuto make an appearance, and each serves for Saiyatasha and for Hututu. Each of them has a wood as his head piece and brings a deer antler in his hand.

This is a Yamuhakto pin/pendant made by Leonard Martza in the mosaic overlay on shell style in the 1970s-1980s. Built with blue turquoise, yellow-lip mother-of-pearl, white mother-of-pearl and black jet, the figure is set on a violet spiny oyster shell. The upper one third of the shell is further decorated by seven green turquoise cabochons. The figure itself measures 0.94 inches tall; the total length of the pin/pendant is 2.33 inches.

Mosaic inlay Yamuhakto pin/pendant, Leonard Martza, LM, 1970s-1980s, 2.33" x 2.37", $800-1200.

Shulawitsi

Shulawitsi or Little Fire God appears first in the Zuni village in the Shalako ceremony. Shulawitsi and his ceremonial father, Shulawitsi An Tachu, make fire with a drill, light the torch of Shulawitsi, and lead the Kachinas to the house south of the Zuni River (Wright, 1985, p. 33).

This Shulawitsi bolo was made by Walter Nahktewa in the flush mosaic inlay style in the 1940s-1950s. It was originally made as a manta pin because it has two small silver loops around the neck on the back. Later, a bolo clasps were added in the 1950s-1960s. He wears a lot of red, blue and white dots all over his body and brings a cedar bark torch in his right hand and two blue-and-black batons in his left. It measures 5.11 inches tall and consists of blue turquoise, red coral, brownish iridescent abalone shell, white mother-of-pearl, and black jet. This Shulawitsi figure should be Walter's representative piece (Ostler et al., 1996, p. 85).

Mosaic inlay Shulawitsi bolo converted from pin, Walter Nahktewa, no hallmark, 1940s-1950s, 2.73" x 5.11", $4000-6000.

Leo Poblano made this Shulawitsi pill box in the mosaic inlay in mother-of-pearl shell style in the 1940s-1950s. The insert measures 0.83 inches wide and 1.39 inches tall. Within this smaller insert the full body portrayal of Shulawitsi is inlaid. The Shulawitsi figure is 1.25 inches tall from the tip of feather to the bottom of his left moccasin. Considering this size, his lapidary skill is far beyond our imagination. The figure consists of blue turquoise, red coral, white mother-of-pearl and black jet. The silver box measures 1.19 inches wide, 1.71 inches long, and 0.84 inches high.

Mosaic inlay Shulawitsi pill box, Leo Poblano, no hallmark, 1940s-1950s, 0.83" x 1.39" for the insert, $1000-1500.

This Shulawitsi bolo was made by Edward Beyuka in the mosaic inlay style on December 28, 2001. I ordered this bolo directly from him when he visited me at the Inn at the Halona. Soon after, he finished its silver work and his son, Jonathan, completed its lapidary work. Like his later pieces, this is a joint work by Edward Beyuka and Jonathan Beyuka. He has a cedar bark torch in his right hand and a blue baton in his left. He wears a fawn-skin bag over his right shoulder. The fawn-skin has a black eye, black nose tip, and yellow ear. It measures 4.77 inches tall and consists of blue turquoise, red coral, dark brown pen shell, yellow-lip mother-of-pearl, white mother-of-pearl, light and dark brown shell, and black jet.

Mosaic inlay Shulawitsi bolo, Edward Beyuka, EAB, 2001, 2.66" x 4.77", $1000-1500.

Dexter Cellicion made this Shulawitsi ring in the mosaic inlay style in the 1950s-1960s. The Shulawitsi head is set on the white mother-of-pearl shell. This ring is made in exactly the same style as Dexter's Hututu ring. The ring face and the figure measure 0.93 inches across and 0.57 inches tall respectively. It consists of blue turquoise, red coral, gold-lip mother-of-pearl, and black jet.

the deer antler base. A lot of colorful dots are inlaid in the mask under which carved turquoise necklace and orange shoulder are set. On top of the mask, a carved dark brown feather is set, and a black-and-white rope is hung. It measures 2.20 inches tall and consists of blue turquoise, red coral, orange spiny oyster, white mother-of-pearl, gold-lip mother-of-pearl, dark brown pen shell, and black mother-of-pearl.

Mosaic inlay Shulawitsi ring, Dexter Cellicion, no hallmark, 1950s-1960s, 0.93" across, $150-225.

Mosaic overlay Shulawitsi bolo, Poncho, 1980s-1990s, 2.20" x 2.20", $200-300.

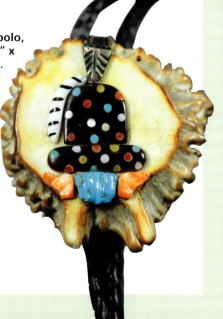

This Shulawitsi bolo was made by a member of the Poncho family in the mosaic overlay style in the 1980s-1990s. It is unique in that the Shulawitsi face is set on

Salimopia

The last Kachina of the Council of Gods or the Saiyatasha party is Salimopia. He is a Warrior Kachina and a guard of the party. There are six Salimopia from each direction, and each year two Salimopia Kachinas from different directions appear as a pair. It is extremely difficult to acquire any Salimopia piece in jewelry. I have only one White Salimopia Bow Guard made by Philander Gia for his step-son. His step-son asked him to make another Kachina Bow Guard and gave the former one back to his step-father. Then, He sold the bow guard to me. Please refer to the pieces made by Philander Gia in the chapter VII of this book.

Koyemshi

Koyemshi or Mud Head is one of the most sacred Zuni Kachinas (Harmsen, 1988, p. 81) and most dangerous of all the Zuni Kachinas (Bunzel, 1984, p. 947). Koyemshi always appears as a full group of 10 members: One Koyemshi father and nine Koyemshi children. They appear in any Kachina Dance ceremony. They are sacred clowns who amuse audiences watching ceremonial dances and help Kachinas to correct their clothing and adornment imperfections caused while dancing.

According to one of my Zuni informants, almost all Koyemshi pieces in Zuni jewelry are not authentic Zuni Koyemshi, but Hopi Koyemshi borrowed by the Zuni. I have 16 Koyemshi pieces, and 12 pieces are the Hopi version of Koyemshi. A Zuni Kachina doll collector and researcher told me that there is a taboo against making a Kachina doll of Koyemshi in Zuni. If one makes an authentic Zuni Koyemshi in a Kachina doll, he or she gets burned in his or her face, or his or her house will be burned.

This Koyemshi bolo was probably made by Leo Poblano in the mosaic inlay in the late 1950s. His body is carved in the convex manner which gives this piece a three-dimensional effect. We can find this kind of style on rare occasions. Only the greatest artists can use this method. It measures 2.64 inches tall and consists of blue turquoise, red coral, pink mussel shell, and black jet. One informant told me he is a Koyemshi priest because he has two feathers in his right hand.

Mosaic inlay Koyemshi bolo, Leo Poblano, no hallmark, 1950s, 1.40" x 2.64", $1000-1500.

Ida Vacit Poblano made this Koyemshi bolo in the mosaic overlay style in the 1950s-1960s. There is a turquoise pin on his left moccasin. It may be a turquoise cluster pin. You can see three round swollen bumps on his head and swollen eyes and mouth in his face. These round bumps can be seen in authentic Zuni Koyemshi as well. It measures 2.20 inches tall and consists of green turquoise, red spiny oyster, pink mussel shell, and black jet.

Mosaic overlay Koyemshi bolo, Ida Vacit Poblano, no hallmark, 1950s-1960s, 1.47" x 2.20", $600-900.

This Koyemshi bolo was made by Ida Vacit Poblano in the mosaic overlay style in the 1950s-1960s. Although there is no bump around the eyes, there are three bumps on the head: one at the top and one on each side of the face. These bumps are set slightly raised. The eye and mouth are dug as round holes, and jet parts are inlaid inside the holes. It measures 2.02 inches tall and consists of green turquoise, red spiny oyster, white mother-of-pearl, and black jet.

Mosaic overlay Koyemshi bolo, Ida Vacit Poblano, no hallmark, 1950s-1960s, 1.09" x 2.02", $500-750.

Dexter Cellicion made this Koyemshi ring in the mosaic inlay style in the 1950s-1960s. The Koyemshi head is set on the white mother-of-pearl shell. This ring is made in exactly the same style as Dexter's Hututu and Shulawitsi rings. The ring face and the figure measure 0.99 inches across and 0.54 inches tall respectively. It consists of brown pipe stone, white mother-of-pearl, and black jet.

Mosaic inlay Koyemshi ring, Dexter Cellicion, no hallmark, 1950s-1960s, 0.99" across, $150-225.

This Koyemshi buckle was made by Augustine Pinto on the mosaic inlay style in the 1950s-1960s. The figure itself measures 1.27 inches tall and consists of blue turquoise, red spiny oyster, pink mussel shell and black jet. The figure is set in the center of the buckle. This figure seems to be made primitively. in each corner of the buckle, an oval turquoise and two silver drops are set, and the wide remaining area is left unset or unstamped. The buckle itself measures 1.41 inches tall.

Mosaic inlay Koyemshi buckle, Augustine Pinto, no hallmark, 1950s-1960s, 2.29" x 1.41", $500-750.

47

The following twelve Koyemshi pieces are made in the Hopi version of Koyemshi characterized by a sharp horn on his head which looks like unicorn's.

This Hopi-style Koyemshi bolo, made in the mosaic inlay in a white clam shell style in the late 1950s to 1960s, is attributed to Dixon and Martha Hustito Shebola by one of my Zuni informants. The clam shell background is concave and cut out in the shape of the design in which colorful parts are inlaid. There is no crack in the background, unlike those usually seen in jet background. The Koyemshi design is different from others and technically complex. I believe this Koyemshi piece is one of the representative Koyemshi designs in Zuni jewelry, along with the one made by Augustine and Rosalie Pinto. This bolo measures 2.45 inches tall and consists of blue turquoise, orange spiny oyster, red coral, black jet, and white clam shell.

Mosaic inlay in clam shell Hopi Koyemshi bolo, Dixon and Martha Hustito Shebola, no hallmark, 1950s-1960s, 1.89" x 2.45", $800-1200.

Dixon Shebola made this Hopi Koyemshi ring in the silver overlay and mosaic inlay style in the 1950s-1960s. The figure is set slightly higher than the silver surface. He has a gourd in his right hand. There are stamps all around the edge of the ring face. The figure itself is 1.01 inches tall and the ring face measures 1.43 inches tall. Considering these measurements, his silver and lapidary works are incredible. It consists of green turquoise, pink coral, and white mother-of-pearl.

Silver overlay and mosaic inlay Hopi Koyemshi ring, Dixon Shebala, no hallmark, 1950s-1960s, 1.05" x 1.43", $200-300.

Augustine and Rosalie Pinto made this Hopi Koyemshi bolo in the mosaic inlay in tortoise shell style in the 1950s-1960s. Although it is not made in their typical raised mosaic inlay style, but with flush inlays, its silver work is in their typical, frequently observed style (Nancy N. Schiffer, 1990, p. 19). This one may have been made before they created their unique raised mosaic inlay style. It measures 1.99 inches tall and consists of blue turquoise, red coral, white mother-of-pearl, black jet, and tortoise shell.

Mosaic inlay Hopi Koyemshi bolo, Augustine Pinto, no hallmark, 1950s-1960s, 1.44" x 1.99", $800-1200.

These three pieces constitute a Hopi Koyemshi set in the raised mosaic inlay in pen shell style in the 1970s-1980s made by Augustine and Rosalie Pinto. Although the necklace and the ring have their "ARP ZUNI" hallmark on the back, the earrings have an "A.R.P. ZUNI" hallmark. They used these two types of hallmarks interchangeably. The latter type of the hallmark is so small that I have to use a magnifier to read it, while the former is easier to read. They became master artists when they established this unique Koyemshi design and the raised mosaic inlay style.

The center piece of the necklace, the ring face, and the earrings without their dangles measure 1.72, 1.44, and 1.24 inches tall respectively. They consist of blue/green turquoise, red coral, white mother-of-pearl, black jet, and brown pen shell. Their Hopi Clown piece is featured later in this book.

Mosaic inlay Hopi Koyemshi earrings, Augustine and Rosalie Pinto, no hallmark, 1970s-1980s, 1.02" x 1.44", $200-300.

Mosaic inlay Hopi Koyemshi necklace, Augustine and Rosalie Pinto, ARP ZUNI, 1970s-1980s, the center piece is 1.23" x 1.72", $600-900.

Mosaic inlay Hopi Koyemshi ring, Augustine and Rosalie Pinto, A. R. P. ZUNI, 1970s-1980s, 0.88" x 1.24", $150-225.

This Koyemshi bracelet in the silver overlay and raised mosaic inlay style in the 1970s-1980s was made by Augustine and Rosalie Pinto. Except for this one, I have never seen another silver overlay piece by them. The center figure and bracelet measure 1.12 and 1.99 inches tall respectively. It consists of blue turquoise, red coral, white mother-of-pearl, black jet, yellow serpentine, and brown pen shell.

None of their Koyemshis has a gourd in his hand.

Silver overlay and mosaic inlay Hopi Koyemshi bracelet, Augustine and Rosalie Pinto, ARP ZUNI, 1970s-1980s, 2.70" x 1.99", $600-900.

Ronnie and Olivia Calavaza made this Zuni Koyemshi bolo in the raised mosaic inlay in pen shell style in the 1980s. At that time, they were still married. The silver plate accepts a lot of stamp work and is encased by colorful stones and shells. This colorful frame is a unique creation of Ronnie and Olivia. This stamped silver plate is cut out in the form of an elongated circle and placed on another plate. The recessed area is blackened, and the Koyemshi figure with the background is set on this area. It is a kind of shadow box style. They made this bolo by combining a couple of styles. This bolo measures 1.60 inches tall and consists of blue turquoise, red coral, white mother-of-pearl, black jet, and brown pen shell.

Mosaic overlay Hopi Koyemshi bolo, Ronnie and Olivia Calavaza, ROC ZUNI, 1980s, 1.43" x 1.60", $300-450.

Beverly Etsate made this Hopi Koyemshi pin/pendant in the raised mosaic inlay style in the 1990s-2000s. As she is a daughter of Augustine and Rosalie Pinto, it should not be surprising that her parents' and Beverly's Koyemshi designs are similar. It measures 1.34 inches tall and consists of blue turquoise, red coral, white mother-of-pearl, black jet, and brown pen shell.

Mosaic overlay Hopi Koyemshi pin/pendant, Beverly Etsate, Bev. Etsate ZUNI NM, 1990s-2000s, 1.11" x 1.34", $80-120.

This seems to be a set of Hopi Koyemshi bracelet and ring, apparently made by the same artist team in the raised mosaic inlay style in the 1980s-1990s. It is very strange that the bracelet has a hallmark of "L. N. & R. C." while the ring has the "C. R. & Paul Luna" hallmark. The Koyemshi design of this set resembles the one made by Augustine and Rosalie Pinto, although the figure wears a bracelet on its right hand and has a gourd in his left hand. The hallmarks, "R. C." and "C. R." might stand for their son, Ronnie Calavaza. The bracelet and ring measure 2.33 and 1.37 inches tall, respectively. They are made of blue turquoise, red coral, white mother-of-pearl, black jet, and dark brown pen shell.

Mosaic overlay Hopi Koyemshi bracelet, artist unknown, L. N. & R. C., 1980s-1990s, 1.72" x 2.33" for the medallion, $400-600.

Mosaic overlay Hopi Koyemshi ring, artist unknown, C. R. & Paul Luna, 1980s-1990s, 1.03" x 1.37" for the medallion, $150-225.

This set of a Hopi Koyemshi bracelet and a ring in the raised mosaic inlay style in the 1970s-1980s was made by an unknown artist. Both have a hallmark: "TW." One of the older artists told me they were made by one of the Weabothees. Although they look very simple for small children or a cheap souvenir piece, the lapidary work is still good. Both of them measure 1.25 inches tall and consist of blue/green turquoise, red coral and white mother-of-pearl.

This Hopi Koyemshi pin/pendant, made by Virgil and Shirley Benn in mosaic inlay style in 2009, is an extremely well made piece that can compete with the best pieces made by the greatest Zuni mosaic artists, such as Leo Poblano and Teddy Weahkee. This figure has a real feeling of dynamic dancing movement. It measures 5.05 inches tall and consists of blue turquoise, red spiny oyster, iridescent abalone, black jet, black mother-of-pearl, and pink shell.

Mosaic inlay Hopi Koyemshi in mother-of-pearl bracelet, artist unknown, TW, 1970s-1980s, 1" x 1.25", $120-180.

Mosaic inlay Hopi Koyemshi in mother-of-pearl ring, artist unknown, TW, 1970s-1980s, 1.08" x 1.32", $60-90.

Mosaic inlay Hopi Koyemshi pin/pendant, Virgil and Shirley Benn, V. & S. Benn, 2009, 2.61" x 5.05", $1000-1500.

III.
Kachinas in the Corn Dance Ceremony

Corn Dance, Rain Dance, and Other Ceremonies

When I asked my Zuni friends to classify Kachina jewelry into categories, they classified many pieces into Corn Dance ceremony and some pieces into Rain Dance ceremony. This way of classification is a little different from the classification seen in the anthropological literature, such as Summer and Winter Dances, Shalako Dance, Winter Solstice Dance, and so on. However, I would like to take the track suggested by my Zuni friends because of its simplicity.

Kachinas in the Corn Dance Ceremony

Many types of Kachina jewelry, such as Antelope Kachina, Ram Kachina, Turkey Kachina, Eagle Kachina, Comanche Kachina, and so on, fall in this category. Out of these, Antelope seems to be made in the highest numbers, and production of Ram Kachina may be second.

Antelope Kachina

Antelope Kachina is classified here as one of the Corn Dance Ceremony participants, although he is classified as part of the mixed dance in the anthropological literature such as *Kachinas of the Zuni* (Wright, 1985, p. 99). Barton Wright notes:

> Mahawe, who is often identified as an elk, is actually antelope...and comes in the Mixed Dance, where he behaves in the same fashion as Deer is usually accompanied by Coyote. He dances for the increase of Antelope and brings rain when he comes.

The Antelope Kachina has been made into jewelry as early as in the 1940-1950s by various artists, including Anthony and Rita Edaakie. Anthony Edaakie established a pattern for Antelope Kachina, and this pattern was given to Andrew Dewa. Anthony's influence on Andrew Dewa, therefore, seems to be evident in Andrew's earlier Antelope pieces.

Frank Vacit made this Antelope Kachina ring in the mosaic overlay style in the 1950s-1960s. It has been confirmed as his by one of his daughters. However, I am not so sure, because he rarely used the overlay style. In spite of this uncertainty of the attribution, this ring is one of the best Antelope pieces, I believe. Its parts are carved and polished individually and are set together, using silver bezels. This method gives each surface curvature. It measures 1.59 inches tall and consists of green turquoise, red spiny oyster, white mother-of-pearl, and black jet.

Mosaic overlay Antelope Kachina ring, Frank Vacit, no hallmark, 1950s-1960s, 0.82" x 1.59", $300-450

This Antelope Kachina bolo was made by an unknown artist in the flush mosaic inlay style in the 1940s-1950s. This inlay method gives the impression of flatness to this bolo, although it is still extremely attractive. It consists of six colors, provided by iridescent abalone, yellow olive shell, and four basic colors of green turquoise, red spiny oyster, white mother-of-pearl, and black jet. This rich variety of colors is unusual for earlier pieces. It measures 1.75 inches tall.

Mosaic inlay Antelope Kachina bolo, artist unknown, no hallmark, 1940s-1950s, 1.57" x 1.75", $600-900.

This Antelope Kachina pendant was made by an unknown artist in the mosaic inlay style in the 1940s-1950s. While its face and collar are raised slightly, the remaining areas are set flat. It measures 1.50 inches tall and consists of green turquoise, red abalone, white mother-of-pearl, and black jet. It is a cute and well executed piece. One of my informants attributed this to Dexter or Roger Cellicion.

Mosaic inlay Antelope Kachina pendant, artist unknown, no hallmark, 1940s-1950s, 0.76" x 1.50", $200-300

On this Antelope bolo, made by an unknown artist in the mosaic inlay style in the 1940s-1950s, the figure is set flush except for the two horns. The horns show curvature on their surface. It measures 2.51 inches tall and consists of blue/green turquoise, red spiny oyster, white mother-of-pearl, and black jet. One of my informants has attributed this to Dexter Cellicion, but I am not so sure about this attribution.

Mosaic overlay Antelope Kachina bolo, artist unknown, no hallmark, 1940s-1950s, 1.18" x 2.51", $300-450.

The following two pieces seem to be made by the same unknown artist.

This Antelope Kachina bolo was made in the mosaic inlay style in the 1940s-1950s. Its bolo clasps are composed of one W-shaped and two round pieces of silver wire. The blue, red, and white head piece and collar are set slightly higher than his face, horns, and shoulder; his black mouth is set much higher than the collar. It measures 1.66 inches tall and consists of blue turquoise, red spiny oyster, white mother-of-pearl, black jet, and iridescent abalone. One informant attributed this bolo to Cachini, while another attributed it to Dexter Cellicion or Andrew Dewa. I am not certain about these attributions.

Mosaic inlay Antelope Kachina bolo, artist unknown, no hallmark, 1940s-1950s, 1.13" x 1.66", $300-450.

The same artist made this Antelope Kachina tie bar in the mosaic inlay style in the 1940s-1950s. The collar and head pieces are set slightly higher than his face and neck, and his mouth is set much higher than the collar. A black dot is inlaid in the white part of the head piece. This dot inlay is frequently seen in the pieces made by great artists such as Leo Poblano and Lambert Homer, Sr. It measures 1.43 inches tall and consists of blue turquoise, red spiny oyster, white mother-of-pearl, black jet and iridescent abalone. This tie bar is attributed to one of the Beyukas by my informant

Mosaic inlay Antelope Kachina tie bar, artist unknown, no hallmark, 1940s-1950s, 0.92" x 1.43", $150-225.

The following three pieces are apparently made by the same artist.

Dexter Cellicion probably made this Antelope Kachina bolo in the mosaic inlay style in the 1940s-1950s. There are many stamped silver drops all around the figure and two W-shaped silver wires for bolo clasps. The figure has triangular eyes and mouth. The triangular mouth is frequently seen in the pieces made by Dexter. It measures 1.73 inches tall and consists of green turquoise, red spiny oyster, white mother-of-pearl, black jet, and iridescent abalone. These stones and shells are individually carved and polished before being set, so the surface is not smooth.

Mosaic inlay Antelope Kachina bolo, Dexter Cellicion, no hallmark, 1940s-1950s, 1.58" x 1.73", $300-450.

This Antelope Kachina pendant with hand-made chain was probably made by Dexter Cellicion in the flush mosaic inlay style in the 1940s-1950s. It measures only 0.92 inches tall. Due to this smaller size, the artist might have selected the flush mosaic inlay style. There are many stamped silver drops all around the face as well. It consists of green turquoise, red spiny oyster, white mother-of-pearl, black jet, and iridescent abalone.

Mosaic inlay Antelope Kachina pendant, Dexter Cellicion, no hallmark, 1940s-1950s, 0.92" x 0.97", $100-150.

Dexter Cellicion also probably made these Antelope Kachina earrings in the 1940s-1950s. They are so tiny that there is no stamped silver drop. Only a few short silver wires are set on both sides of the colorful head piece. It measures 0.84 inches tall and consists of blue turquoise, red spiny oyster, white mother-of-pearl, black jet and iridescent abalone.

Mosaic inlay Antelope Kachina earrings, Dexter Cellicion, no hallmark, 1940s-1950s, 0.68" x 0.84", $200-300.

Dexter and Eva Cellicion made this Antelope Kachina Pendant in the 1970s-1980s. The piece was made first in the mosaic inlay style and set in the white mother-of-pearl background. They are set on the silver backing, and silver wires are welded around the figure and the back-ground. Furthermore, the plain parts of the silver backing are cut out, and silver dangles are set. As to the mosaic inlay work, the triangular mouth, collar, ears, and colorful head piece are set slightly above the face. Thus, it is made in an extremely complex manner. The figure itself measures 0.98 inches tall and consists of blue turquoise, red spiny oyster, white mother-of-pearl, and black jet and green serpentine.
The total length of the pendant excluding dangles is 1.83 inches tall.

Mosaic overlay Antelope Kachina pendant, Dexter and Eva Cellicion, Dexter & Eva Cellicion Zuni New Mexico, 1970s-1980s, 1.45" x 1.83", $300-450.

The following three older pieces are apparently made by the same artist. They are confirmed as Robert Cachini Sr.'s pieces by his sister, Sybil Cachini.

This Antelope pin/pendant was made in the mosaic inlay style on a gold-lip mother-of-pearl shell in the 1960s by Robert Cachini, Sr. An almost identical piece is featured in *Zuni Jewelry* (Bassman, 1992, 29) and is attributed to Sybil Cachini. The collar and head pieces are set slightly higher than the face and horns. The figure measures 1.06 inches tall and consists of blue turquoise, white mother-of-pearl, black jet, green serpentine, and gold-lip mother-of-pearl. The pin/pendant without dangles measures 2.44 inches tall.

Robert Cachini, Sr., made this Antelope Kachina bracelet in the mosaic inlay style in the 1960s. The collar and head piece are set slightly higher than the face. The central figure measures 1.99 inches tall and consists of blue turquoise, red spiny oyster, white mother-of-pearl, yellow-lip mother-of-pearl, black jet, and green serpentine.

Mosaic overlay Antelope Kachina bracelet, Robert Cachini Sr., no hallmark, 1960s, 1.40" x 1.99" for the central piece,, $400-600.

Mosaic overlay Antelope Kachina pendant, Robert Cachini Sr., no hallmark, 1960s, 2.38" x 2.44", $200-300.

This Antelope Kachina ring was made by Robert Cachini, Sr., in the mosaic inlay style in the 1960s. The collar and the neck piece are set slightly higher than the face as well. It measures 0.84 inches tall and consists of blue turquoise, white mother-of-pearl, gold-lip mother-of-pearl, black jet, and green serpentine.

Mosaic inlay Antelope Kachina ring, Robert Cachini Sr., no hallmark, 1960s, 0.78" x 0.84", $100-150.

An Antelope Kachina ring in the mosaic inlay style in the 1960s is confirmed to be by made by Robert Cachini, Sr., by Sybil Cachini. The black-and-white mouth and collar, colorful head piece, upper chest, ears, and two horns are set higher than the face and eagle feather. The figure measures 1.12 inches tall and consists of green turquoise, red coral, white mother-of-pearl, and black jet and brown pen shell. The year this ring was made might be located between the dates of the three pieces just described and the following ring.

Mosaic inlay Antelope Kachina ring, Robert Cachini Sr., no hallmark, 1960s, 0.67" x 1.11" for the figure, $150-225.

Robert Cachini, Sr., made this Antelope Kachina ring in the mosaic inlay style in the 1970s. Although his small pieces are marked "R. C. Sr. ZUNI" in the 1970s and on, this ring has no hallmark. All parts of the figure are individually carved and polished before being set in the silver channels. This technique gives this figure a three-dimensional appearance. A black-and-white mouth is set higher than other parts. It measures 1.22 inches tall and consists of blue turquoise, red coral, white mother-of-pearl, black jet, and gold lip mother-of-pearl.

Mosaic inlay Antelope Kachina ring, Robert Cachini Sr., no hallmark, 1970s, 0.79" x 1.22", $150-225.

This Antelope Kachina ring was made by Sybil Cachini in the mosaic inlay style in the 1980s-1990s. It is extremely tiny, measuring only 0.70 inches tall. It consists of green turquoise, red coral, white mother-of-pearl, black jet, and gold lip mother-of-pearl.

Mosaic inlay Antelope Kachina ring, Sybil Cachini, CACHINI, 1980s-1990s, 0.39" x 0.70", $60-90.

Anthony and Rita Edaakie made this Antelope Kachina bolo in the mosaic overlay style in the 1940s-1950s. Vertical lines are carved on the green collar which is designed as a white fir branch. A part of the head piece is carved vertically as well. These are set slightly higher than the face, and a black mouth is set much higher. The lapidary work of the chest is especially well made: Four thin black jet parts are inserted between two different colored parts respectively, and one more thin turquoise is added between red and black parts. The face, head, collar, and chest are fastened on the silver backing with one long silver plate, while black horns are set on the silver backing separately. One bumped silver plate, representing an eagle feather, is set between the horns, and two similar plates are set on the both sides of the face. Moreover, eight stamped silver drops are set symmetrically. It measures 2.16 inches tall and consists of blue/green turquoise, red spiny oyster, white mother-of-pearl, black jet, and a cowrie shell.

Mosaic overlay Antelope Kachina bolo, Anthony and Rita Edaakie, no hallmark, 1940s-1950s, 1.60" x 2.16", $400-600.

This Antelope Kachina bolo, made by Anthony and Rita Edaakie in the mosaic overlay style in the 1940s-1950s, is almost identical with the bolo described just above, although the lapidary work of this bolo is simpler. It measures 1.54 inches tall and consists of blue turquoise, red spiny oyster, white mother-of-pearl, and black jet.

Mosaic overlay Antelope Kachina bolo, Anthony and Rita Edaakie, no hallmark, 1940s-1950s, 1.54" x 2.15", $400-600.

Anthony and Rita Edaakie made this Antelope Kachina ring in the mosaic inlay style in the 1950s-1960s. Its head piece looks simple compared with the bolos just described. Although it does not look three-dimensional, all surfaces are not flat and have curvature. It is an old style of mosaic overlay/inlay. In addition, there are stamped and unstamped silver drops all around the figure. The stamped silver drops are the same as the ones seen in the bolos just described. It measures 1.79 inches tall and consists of blue turquoise, red coral, white mother-of-pearl, black jet, and iridescent abalone.

Mosaic inlay Antelope Kachina ring, Anthony and Rita Edaakie, no hallmark, 1950s-1960s, 1.22" x 1.79", $200-300.

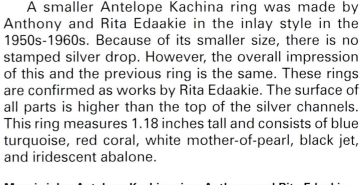

A smaller Antelope Kachina ring was made by Anthony and Rita Edaakie in the inlay style in the 1950s-1960s. Because of its smaller size, there is no stamped silver drop. However, the overall impression of this and the previous ring is the same. These rings are confirmed as works by Rita Edaakie. The surface of all parts is higher than the top of the silver channels. This ring measures 1.18 inches tall and consists of blue turquoise, red coral, white mother-of-pearl, black jet, and iridescent abalone.

Mosaic inlay Antelope Kachina ring, Anthony and Rita Edaakie, no hallmark, 1950s-1960s, 0.87" x 1.18", $150-225.

Andrew Dewa made this Antelope Kachina necklace in the mosaic overlay style in the 1970s-1980s. This Antelope figure looks strange. It has unusual horns on both sides of the face that are similar with the horns of Ram Kachina along with the usual antelope horns. The black ears, black-and-white collar, and blue necklace are set higher than the head piece, face, side horns, and upper chest, and the horns and a feather are set lower than all the other parts. The design of the side medallions of the necklace may be taken from the ornament over the head piece of his Ram Kachina jewelry. The central figure measures 2.84 inches tall and consists of blue turquoise, red coral, white mother-of-pearl, black jet, and iridescent abalone.

Mosaic overlay Antelope Kachina necklace, Andrew Dewa, A. DEWA ZUNI, 1970s-1980s, 1.57" x 2.84" for the center piece, $1000-1500.

This Antelope Kachina pin/pendant was made by Andrew Dewa in the mosaic overlay style in the 1960s. It is clearly his work although there is no hallmark. The stamped silver drops and a stamped silver plate on the bottom are identical with those of the next bracelet. Its face looks narrower than his later pieces. It measures 1.85 inches tall and consists of blue turquoise, red coral, white mother-of-pearl, black jet, and dark brown pen shell.

Mosaic overlay Antelope Kachina pin/pendant, Andrew Dewa, no hallmark, 1960s, 1.20" x 1.85", $200-300.

This Antelope Kachina bracelet, made by Andrew Dewa in the mosaic overlay style in the 1970s-1980s, should be one of his representative pieces. Please notice its intricate head piece and traditional dress. The head piece has a cloud symbol in it. His lapidary skill should be appraised as one of the best. The figure measures 3.67 inches tall and consists of blue turquoise, red coral, white mother-of-pearl, and black jet, along with gold lip mother-of-pearl and dark brown pen shell.

Mosaic overlay Antelope Kachina Bracelet, Andrew Dewa, A. DEWA ZUNI, 1960s-1970s, 2.11" x 3.67" for the central medallion, $1200-1800.

Vera Luna made this Antelope Kachina pin in the mosaic inlay style in the 1970s-1980s. The black part in the face above the mouth is rare and seen in Plate 31 of *Kachinas of The Zuni* (Wright, 1985, p. 100). The figure has a stick-out mouth, a carved collar designed like white fir leaves, and a colorful head piece. It has three feathers between the horns as well. It measures 1.75 inches tall and consists of blue turquoise, red coral, white mother-of-pearl, black jet, and green serpentine.

Mosaic overlay Antelope Kachina pin, Vera Luna, V L, 1970s-1980s, 0.94" x 1.72", $200-300.

This is an Antelope Kachina ring made by an unknown artist in the mosaic inlay style in the 1970s-1980s. It is signed "BW," using electric pen. It is made in the flush inlay technique. It measures 1.46 inches tall and consists of green turquoise, red coral, white mother-of-pearl, and black jet. The deep green material for the collar is unknown.

Mosaic inlay Antelope Kachina ring, artist unknown, BW, 1970s-1980s, 1.16" x 1.46", $80-120.

This Antelope Kachina pendant in the mosaic inlay in mother-of-pearl shell style in the 1970s-1980s is by an unknown artist. It is stamped: "Lorenzo," which is the name of the silversmith who did the silver work on this pendant. However, whether he is also a lapidary or not is uncertain. As to its lapidary, one informant attributed it to Alonzo Hustito, while another informant to Leonard Lonjose. Martin and Esther Panteah made a similar design as well (Bell and McQueary, 1976, p. 56). The mother-of-pearl medallion measures 1.58 inches tall and total length of the pendant is 2.38 inches long. It consists of blue turquoise, red spiny oyster, white mother-of-pearl, yellow shell, and brown pen shell. The medallion is encircled by nineteen ox blood corals.

Mosaic inlay Antelope Kachina pendant, artist unknown, Lorenzo, 1970s-1980s, 1.96" x 2.38", $300-450.

This Female Antelope Kachina bolo was probably made by Walter Nahktewa in the mosaic overlay style in the 1940s-1950s. It is an unusual Kachina that rarely appears as a jewelry piece. The design of the head piece and the black part of the upper face are rarely seen. A black-and-white mouth sticks out highly. The bolo tips may depict his kilt and sash in a miniature size. Please refer to the Antelope bow guard made by Leo Poblano in 1948 (Ostler et al., 1996, p. 101). There is a similarity between his bow guard and this bolo. Walter Nahktewa should be evaluated as highly as Leo Poblano, Lambert Homer, Sr., Frank Vacit and Teddy Weahkee. This bolo slide measures 2.64 inches tall and consists of blue turquoise, red spiny oyster, white mother-of-pearl, and black jet.

Mosaic inlay Female Antelope Kachina bolo, Walter Nahktewa, no hallmark, 1940s-1950s, 2.12" x 2.64", $3000-4500.

Ram Kachina

It is also called the Mountain Sheep Kachina or the Big-Horned Kachina. His full figure was depicted by Duane Dishta (Wright, 1985, p. 100).

Andrew Dewa made this Ram Kachina bolo in the mosaic overlay style in the 1960s. There is a big horn made of tortoise shell, which is a signifying feature for Ram Kachina. It is a profile of the Ram Kachina with a colorful head piece, face, and upper body of the ceremonial garment. Stamped silver drops and stamped silver wire on the bottom edge are the same as those on his previously introduced older Antelope Kachina piece. There are two eagle feathers and a colorful ornament over the head piece. This should be one of the most magnificent art works made by Andrew Dewa. It measures 4.34 inches tall and consists of blue turquoise, red coral, white mother-of-pearl, black jet, gold lip mother-of-pearl, and iridescent abalone.

Mosaic overlay Ram Kachina Bolo, Andrew Dewa, A. DEWA ZUNI, 1960s, 2.65" x 4.34", $1200-1800.

This Ram Kachina bolo was made by Andrew Dewa in the mosaic overlay style in the late 1960s-1980s. As there is no antelope horn but two curled horns, this is a Ram Kachina. The stamped silver drops and the stamped silver platelet on the bottom edge are the same as those of his Antelope Kachina necklace in this book. It measures 3.02 inches tall and consists of green turquoise, red coral, white mother-of-pearl, black jet, gold lip mother-of-pearl, and iridescent abalone.

Mosaic overlay Ram Kachina Bolo, Andrew Dewa, A. DEWA ZUNI, 1960s-1980s, 1.46" x 3.02", $800-1200.

This Ram Kachina ring, made by Robert Cachini, Sr., in the mosaic inlay style in the 1970s-1980s, is hallmarked "R. C. Sr. ZUNI." The similar piece is featured in *Hallmarks of the Southwest* (Wright, 2000, on the second photo page before the Contents page). The caption says only "R. C. Sr," but the initials stand for Robert Cachini, Sr. The ring shown here is a small but well-made piece that has a three-dimensional effect. It measures 1.10 inches tall and consists of blue/green turquoise, red coral, white mother-of-pearl, gold lip mother-of-pearl, and black jet.

Mosaic inlay Ram Kachina ring, Robert Cachini Sr., R. C. Sr. ZUNI, 1970s-1980s, 0.95" x 1.10", $200-300.

The following three pieces constitute a set made by Robert Cachini, Sr., in the mosaic inlay style in the 1970s-1980s.

The Ram Kachina necklace is hallmarked "Robert Cachini Sr." on the back of the center piece. We can clearly see channels. For example, the head piece consists of seven parts, and they are combined together, carved, polished, and set in a channel. The face, collar and upper chest are done in the same way as the head piece. The center piece and side pieces measure 2.04 and 1.38 inches tall, respectively. It consists of green turquoise, red coral, white mother-of-pearl, and black jet.

The matching Ram Kachina ring, complementing the necklace, is hallmarked "R. C. Sr. Zuni" with an electric pen. Although the mosaic inlay pattern of this ring is exactly the same as the necklace, red color used in this ring does not match that of the necklace. It measures 1.17 inches long and consists of green turquoise, red and pink coral, white mother-of-pearl, and black jet.

The Ram Kachina earrings have no hallmark on their back. However, they seem to be perfectly matched with the ring. Each earring measures 1.04 inch tall.

The surfaces of these earrings and ring look rounder than that of the center piece of the necklace, probably because of their smaller size.

Mosaic overlay Ram Kachina necklace, Robert Cachini Sr., R. C. Sr. ZUNI, 1970s-1980s, 1.81" x 2.04" for the center piece, $600-900.

Mosaic overlay Ram Kachina ring, Robert Cachini Sr., no hallmark, 1970s-1980s, 0.93" x 1.17", $200-300.

Mosaic overlay Ram Kachina earrings, Robert Cachini Sr., no hallmark, 1970s-1980s, 0.85" x 1.04", $300-450.

This Ram Kachina bolo, made by Sybil Cachini in the mosaic inlay style in 2011, looks flatter than the pieces made by her brother, Robert Cachini, Sr. It measures 2.65 inches long and consists of blue turquoise, red coral, white mother-of-pearl, and black jet.

This is a Ram Kachina pendant made by Sybil Cachini in the mosaic inlay style in 2011. It measures 1.39 inches tall and consists of synthesized opal, red coral, white mother-of-pearl, and black jet.

Mosaic overlay Ram Kachina pendant, Sybil Cachini, Sybil Cachini, 2011, 1.14" x 1.39", $100-150.

Mosaic overlay Ram Kachina bolo, Sybil Cachini, Sybil Cachini ZUNI. NM., 2011, 2.03" x 2.65", $300-450.

71

Beverly Etsate made this Ram Kachina pendant in the raised mosaic overlay in the 1990s. The whole body of the figure is set inside the dark brown pen shell. It measures 1.54 inches tall and consists of blue turquoise, red coral, white mother-of-pearl, gold lip mother-of-pearl, and black jet.

This Ram Kachina pendant, made by Beverly Etsate in the raised mosaic overlay style in the 1990s, measures 1.33 inches long and consists of blue turquoise, red coral, white mother-of-pearl, gold lip mother-of-pearl, and black jet.

Mosaic overlay Ram Kachina pendant, Beverly Etsate, Bev. Etsate ZUNI. NM, 1990s, 1.31" x 1.54", $80-120.

Mosaic overlay Ram Kachina pendant, Beverly Etsate, Bev. Etsate ZUNI. NM, 1990s, 1.08" x 1.33", $60-90.

Turkey Kachina

The profile of Whole Turkey Kachina was drawn by Duane Dishta (Wright, 1985, p. 101). On the same page, Wright says:

> The Turkey Kachina, Tone-ah...appears in the Mixed Dance and seems to be merely one of the representations of animals and has no unusual attributes.

Thus, Wright does not describe any special attribute on either the Turkey Kachina or the Ram Kachina.

This Turkey Kachina bolo, made by Myra Tucson in the mosaic inlay style in the 1940s-1950s, is all flush and has no bump on the bolo slide. There are fan-shaped brown feathers over the head and two triangular ornaments above the ears. These triangular ornaments may represent squash blossoms. They are characteristic of this Kachina design. There are two W-shaped bolo clasps on the back, and the bolo has two bolo tips of white-and-brown feathers. The forehead has four feathers for ornamentation, and the upper face has three sets of ornamentation. Each set is made up of two crescents. It measures 1.77 inches tall and consists of blue turquoise, red coral, white mother-of-pearl, black jet, brown tortoise shell, and iridescent abalone.

Mosaic inlay Turkey Kachina bolo, Myra Tucson, no hallmark, 1940s-1950s, 1.96" x 1.77", $1000-1500.

This Turkey Kachina bolo, probably made by Dexter Cellicion in the mosaic inlay style in the 1950s-1960s, has two triangular ornaments over the ears and fan-shaped feathers over the head, like the one just described. The triangular mouth is characteristic to Dexter's various Kachina figures. There is one red and blue ornament in the center position of the brown and white feathers. It measures 2.82 inches tall and consists of blue turquoise, red coral, white mother-of-pearl, black jet, and green serpentine.

Mosaic inlay Turkey Kachina bolo, Dexter Cellicion, no hallmark, 1950s-1960s, 2.57" x 2.82", $600-900.

Dexter and Eva Cellicion made this Turkey Kachina in the raised mosaic style in the 1970s-1980s. This provides a more refined figure than the previous one because its lapidary work is smoother, shinier, and more three-dimensional. There are triangular ornaments over the ears and two red and green feathers are located between two black and white feathers. It measures 2.17 inches tall and consists of blue turquoise, red coral, white mother-of-pearl, black jet, and green abalone.

Mosaic inlay Turkey Kachina bolo, Dexter and Eva Cellicion, Dexter & Eva Cellicion Zuni N. Mex., 1970s-1980s, 1.75" x 2.17", $400-600.

This Kachina pin was made by Dexter Cellicion in the mosaic inlay style in the 1950s-1960s. Its characteristic feature is Kachina's turquoise part sticking out in the center of the face. It reminds me of the similar part of the Bee Kachina, Antelope Kachina, or Turkey Kachina (Wright, 1985, pp. 98-101). Although there is no rectangular ornament over the ear, it might be a Turkey Kachina. One informant calls it a Turkey Dancer, while another simply calls it a Corn Dancer. It measures 2.33 inches tall and consists of blue/green turquoise, red spiny oyster, white mother-of-pearl, and black jet.

Mosaic inlay Kachina pin, Dexter Cellicion, no hallmark, 1950s-1960s, 2.31" x 2.33", $600-900.

Wotemthla Kachina

Wotemthla is a Kachina who appears in the Mixed Dance, sometimes together with Red Beard Kachina. He has a long snout, is adorned with the eagle feathers on the back of his mask, and wears a fur around his shoulders.

Frank Vacit made this Wotemthla bolo in the silver overlay and mosaic inlay style in the 1940s-1950s. It has his "ear of corn" hallmark on the back. The big red ears and black and white eagle feathers resemble those of the Corn Kachina or Wotemthla Kachina made by Dexter Cellicion. It measures 1.46 inches tall and consists of green turquoise, red abalone, white mother-of-pearl, and black jet.

Silver overlay/mosaic inlay Wotemthla Kachina bolo, Frank Vacit, his "ear of corn" hallmark, 1950s-1960s, 1.83" x 2.03", $1000-1500.

This Wotemthla Kachina ring was made by Frank Vacit in the silver overlay/mosaic inlay in the 1950s-1960s. The big red ears and turquoise feathers may suggest it is the same Kachina being depicted in the aforementioned bolo. The ring face measures 1.11 inches tall, and the figure consists of blue/green turquoise, red spiny oyster, white mother-of-pearl, black jet, a yellow shell, and black mother-of-pearl.

Silver overlay/mosaic inlay Wotemthla Kachina ring, Frank Vacit, his "ear of corn" hallmark, 1950s-1960s, 0.79" x 1.11", $200-300.

This Wotemthla Kachina pendant was made by an unknown artist in the mosaic inlay in mother-of-pearl style in the 1950s-1960s. The length of the figure is only 0.84 inches. In spite of its smaller size, the lapidary work is incredibly intricate. Look at the stepped mouth! Its silver work is intricate as well. The size of the pendant face is 1.14 inches, and the figure consists of blue turquoise, red coral, white mother-of-pearl, black jet, black mother-of-pearl, green serpentine, and a yellow shell. One informant has attributed it to Dexter Cellicion, but I am not sure about this attribution.

Mosaic inlay in mother of pearl Wotemthla Kachina pendant, artist unknown, no hallmark, 1950s-1960s, 1.22" x 1.43", $100-150.

This Wotemthla Kachina pendant made in the mosaic inlay in mother-of-pearl style in the 1950s-1960s is by the same unknown artist described just above. The mouth is apparently in the stepped-cloud form. The pendant face is 1.15 inches tall, and the figure consists of blue turquoise, red coral, white mother-of-pearl, black jet, and iridescent abalone. This pendant lacks a silver wire decoration on the bottom.

Mosaic inlay in mother-of-pearl Wotemthla Kachina pendant, artist unknown, no hallmark, 1950s-1960s, 1.14" x 1.42", $100-150.

Sybil Cachini made these Wotemthla Kachina earrings in the mosaic inlay stile in the 1990s-2000s. Each earring is very tiny (0.77 inches tall). Considering this smaller size, her lapidary and silver works are excellent. I asked her what kind of Kachina he was. She replied, "Wotemthla." I further asked the English name for Wotemthla, and she told me, "Just a Kachina." The figure consists of blue turquoise, red coral, white mother-of-pearl, and black jet.

Mosaic inlay Wotemthla Kachina earrings, Sybil Cachini, Cachini, 1990s-2000s, 0.53" x 0.77", $50-75.

Eagle Kachina

Eagle Kachina appears as a side dancer in the Hillili Dance (Wright, 1985, pp. 111-112). One informant says that he appears in the winter Hillili and Corn Dances. The Eagle Kachina with a mask is different from the Eagle Dancer with an eagle cap. I would say the most famous and well-made Eagle Kachina is the one made by Bruce Zunie (Ostler et al., 1996, p. 84).

This Eagle Kachina bolo, made by Frank Vacit in the silver overlay and mosaic inlay style in the 1950s-1960s, depicts the back of the Kachina with his head turned to his left. In the left corner of the bolo, a part of the Rain Bird design is added. It measures 2.32 inches tall and consists of green turquoise, red coral, white mother-of-pearl, black jet, and brown pen shell.

Silver overlay and mosaic inlay Eagle Kachina bolo, Frank Vacit, no hallmark, 1950s-1960s, 1.89" x 2.32", $1200-1800.

Frank Vacit made this Eagle Kachina bolo in the silver overlay and mosaic inlay style in the 1950s-1960s. It is almost identical with the bolo described just above, except for the color combinations of feathers over their heads. Frank Vacit made this design until the 1990s.

Silver overlay and mosaic inlay Eagle Kachina bolo, Frank Vacit, no hallmark, 1950s-1960s, 1.88" x 2.31", $1200-1800.

The Eagle Kachina bolo on the next page was made by Frank Vacit in the mosaic inlay in tortoise shell style in the 1950s-1960s. One of Frank's daughters told me that a friend in California sent Frank a whole tortoise shell and he used it for silver.

As the tools and technique used for cutting out tortoise shell are identical with those for silver overlay, he might have applied them to this tortoise shell work. However, the Kennedy Collection digital archive attributes an almost identical piece to Dan Simplicio. This bolo has bolo tips which depict a part of the Rain Bird design seen in the lower left corner of the two Eagle Kachina bolos described just above. They enhance this bolo's attractiveness. It measures 2.53 inches tall and consists of green turquoise, red coral, white mother-of-pearl, and black jet.

Mosaic inlay in tortoise shell Eagle Kachina bolo, Frank Vacit, no hallmark, 1950s-1960s, 2.06" x 2.53", $1200-1800.

Frank Vacit made this Eagle Kachina buckle in the mosaic inlay in tortoise shell style in the 1950s-1960s. The figure is smaller (1.50 inches tall) than that of the bolo just described (2.10 inches tall). The buckle measures 2.06 inches tall and consists of green turquoise, red coral, white mother-of-pearl, and black jet.

Mosaic inlay in tortoise shell Eagle Kachina buckle, Frank Vacit, no hallmark, 1950s-1960s, 1.82" x 2.06", $800-1200.

This Eagle Kachina pin/pendant was made by Frank Vacit in the mosaic inlay in tortoise shell style in the 1950s-1960s. It is very small (1.53 inches tall including its silver edge) and consists of green turquoise, red coral, white mother-of-pearl, and black jet.

This and the two previous Vacit pieces face to their right while two silver overlay/mosaic inlay bolos made by Frank Vacit face to their left.

Mosaic inlay in tortoise shell Eagle Kachina pin/pendant, Frank Vacit, no hallmark, 1950s-1960s, 1.24" x 1.53", $300-450.

This Eagle Kachina pin/pendant, probably made by Porfilio Sheyka in the mosaic inlay style in the 1980s-1990s, is almost identical to a bolo featured as thunderbird in *Ray Manley's Southwestern Arts & Crafts* (Ray Manley, 1975, 24). However, the face is apparently an Eagle Kachina. This pin has no hallmark but an inscription of "Zuni." Sheyka's animal pieces seem to always bear his hallmark; therefore, my attribution is not finalized. The absence of the hallmark might make this design controversial. This pin has a face of the Eagle Kachina, Cloud-and Rain symbol in its body, wings, and a tail. The stamped silver work is unique. It measures 2.26 inches tall and consists of blue turquoise, red coral, white mother-of-pearl, gold lip mother-of-pearl, and black jet.

Mosaic inlay Eagle Kachina pin/pendant, Porfilio Sheyka, no hallmark, 1980s-1990s, 2.50" x 2.26", $300-450.

This Eagle Kachina bolo/pendant, probably made by Porfilio Sheyka in the 1980s-1990s, has two matching bolo tips, each depicting the same Eagle Kachina face. The ceremonial garments are so elaborately made that this bolo becomes a colorful piece. It measures 2.77 inches tall and consists of blue turquoise, red coral, white mother-of-pearl, a yellow shell, and a grey translucent material for ornament over the head.

Mosaic inlay Eagle Kachina bolo, Porfilio Sheyka, no hallmark 1980s-1990s, 3.57" x 2.77", $500-750.

Porfilio Sheyka probably made this Eagle Kachina bolo in the mosaic inlay style in the 1970s-1980s. It has a scratched ZUNI and a broken arrow hallmark. An almost identical bolo is featured along with two other pieces as the Arizona Highways Hall of Fame pieces (*Arizona Highways*, August 1974, p. 32). These two other pieces are attributed to Porfilio, while the Eagle Kachina bolo is of the "artist unknown." The piece below measures 3.56 inches tall and consists of blue turquoise, red coral, white mother-of-pearl, gold lip mother-of-pearl and black jet.

Mosaic inlay Eagle Kachina bolo, Porfilio Sheykaa, broken arrow and ZUNI, 1970s-1980s, 4.99" x 3.56", $600-900.

Bear Kachina

There are two types of Bear Kachina in Zuni: the Kachina with an upper half of the body looking like a real bear and the other with the Bear Kachina mask on (Wright, 1985, pp. 101-102).

This Bear Kachina bolo was made by Andrea Lonjose Shirley in the mosaic inlay in 2003. I bought it directly from her. He has a gourd in his right hand and a yucca bundle in his left hand. His right knee is raised high so his left foot can just be seen. Andrea's lapidary work is perfectly done. However, I would appreciate a feeling of movement even more if this piece were built like the works of her mentors, Virgil and Shirley Benn. It measures 3.52 inches tall and consists of blue turquoise, red coral, white mother-of-pearl, gold lip mother-of-pearl, dark green malachite, iridescent abalone, and black jet.

Mosaic inlay Bear Kachina bolo, Andrea Lonjose, ALS, 2003, 1.44" x 3.52", $300-450.

Comanche Kachina

There are two types of Comanche dancer: The one with the mask on and the other with his face unpainted. According to my Zuni friend, the former is the Comanche Kachina. The latter belongs to the category of Social Dancers, who have less religious meaning.

Dexter and Rosemary Cellicion probably made this Comanche Kachina bolo in the mosaic inlay style in the 1950s-1960s. A war bonnet and painting around the eye and on nose and mouth signify that this figure is a Comanche Kachina. If a Kachina wears some feathers over the head, he might be an Apache Kachina. As to the lapidary work of this piece, stones and shells are set slightly higher than the top walls of the silver channels, and their edges are carved to make them round. Consequently, the figure looks three-dimensional. It measures 3.56 inches tall and consists of green turquoise, red/orange spiny oyster, white mother-of-pearl, iridescent abalone, dark brown pen shell, and light brown stone or shell.

Mosaic inlay Comanche Kachina bolo, Dexter and Rosemary Cellecion, no hallmark, 1950s-1960s, 2.79" x 3.56", $800-1200.

This Comanche Kachina bolo was probably made by Dexter and Rosemary Cellicion in the mosaic inlay style in the 1950s-1960s. As the stones are all set flat, it should be called the flush mosaic inlay. Although blue, white, and dark brown dominate this figure, a small red dot in his cheek makes this figure more attractive. It measures 3.56 inches tall and consists of blue turquoise, red coral, white mother-of-pearl, and dark brown pen shell.

Mosaic inlay Comanche Kachina bolo, Dexter and Rosemary Cellicion, no hallmark, 1950s-1960s, 2.73" x 3.69", $1000-1500.

Dexter and Rosemary Cellicion also probably made this Comanche Kachina bracelet in the flush mosaic inlay style in the 1950s-1960s. Although the design of the head band and the color combination as a whole are different from those of the bolo just described, the basic design is totally the same. Based on this fact, we can safely say it is made by the same artist: Ralph Quam. Similar feather ornament is added behind the bonnet and this addition makes this bracelet special. The central figure measures 3.68 inches tall and consists of blue turquoise, red coral, white mother-of-pearl, gold lip mother-of-pearl, and dark brown pen shell.

Mosaic inlay Comanche Kachina bracelet, Dexter and Rosemary Cellicion, no hallmark, 1950s-1960s, 3.07" x 3.68", $1000-1500.

Dexter and Mary Ann Cellicion made this Comanche Kachina bolo in the mosaic inlay style in the 1960s. The figure itself is made in the mosaic inlay style and then set on the tortoise shell backed with the heavy silver plate. The tortoise shell background is framed with silver plates, and both sides are stamped using dies. All feathers are carved in order to look like real feathers. The silver drops around the figure on the tortoise shell remind me of Dexter Cellicion's newer Antelope Kachina pendant. The figure measures 1.54 inches tall, excluding the silver drops, and consists of blue/green turquoise, red coral, red spiny oyster, white mother-of-pearl, green serpentine, and a light brown melon shell.

Mosaic inlay Comanche Kachina on tortoise shell bolo, Dexter and Mary Ann Cellicion, no hallmark, 1950s-1960s, 2.26" x 3.00", $600-900.

This Comanche Kachina bolo, made by Dexter Cellicion in the mosaic inlay style in the 1960s, has a vertically stamped D/C hallmark, which stands for Dexter Cellicion. This figure is almost identical to the bolo just described. All inlaid parts are set higher than the top of the channel wall and the feathers are carved in order to look realistic. It measures 2.03 inches tall and consists of blue turquoise, red coral, white mother-of-pearl, black jet, iridescent abalone, and light brown melon shell.

Mosaic inlay Comanche Kachina bolo, Dexter and Mary Ann Cellicion, D/C stamped vertically, 1960s, 1.38" x 2.03", $400-600.

A Comanche Kachina buckle made by Dexter and Mary Ann Cellicion in the mosaic inlay style in the 1960s. The Comanche Kachina head is set in the center of the buckle and, both sides of the buckle are inlaid with rectangular parts of four colors. The remaining area is inlaid with tortoise shell. It measures 3.21 inches wide and 2.05 inches tall and consists of blue turquoise, red coral, white mother-of-pearl, spotted cowrie shell, and black jet.

Mosaic inlay Comanche Kachina buckle, Dexter and Mary Ann Cellicion, no hallmark, 1960s, 3.21" x 2.05", $600-900.

This Comanche Kachina ring was made by Dexter and Mary Ann Cellicion in the mosaic inlay style in the 1960s. The surface is all flush, and it has an original tag, showing the price of $54. It measures 1.23 inches tall and consists of blue turquoise, dark red coral, white mother-of-pearl, black jet, and iridescent abalone.

Mosaic inlay Comanche Kachina ring, Dexter and Mary Ann Cellicion, no hallmark, 1960s, 1.02" x 1.23", $80-120.

These Comanche Kachina watch tips were probably made by Dexter and Mary Ann Cellicion in the mosaic inlay style in the 1960s. Since these figures and the figure of the ring just described are so similar, I have considered that these watch tips might also be the Cellicions' works. The figures without bails measure 1.15 inches tall and consists of blue turquoise, red coral, white mother-of-pearl, white clam shell, and black jet.

Mosaic inlay Comanche Kachina watch tips, Dexter Cellicion, no hallmark, 1960s, 0.87" x 1.15", $120-180.

IV.
Kachinas in the Rain Dance and Other Ceremonies

Another main Ceremony is that of the Rain Dance. It is held from mid-June until mid-September. At the end of this Summer Dance, the corn grinding ceremony might be held. During the Winter Solstice ceremonies and the Corn Dance ceremony, the Ground-Cleansing Ceremony may be held. Furthermore, in the Mixed Dance, various Kachinas dance together. If this Mixed Dance is held during night, it will be called the Night Dance, which starts at about 10 PM and lasts until 2 or 3 AM. It is truly a gorgeous dance performed in the end of the Winter Dance.

Kachinas in the Rain Dance Ceremony

The main performer of the Rain Dance ceremony is Kokokshi or "Beautiful or Good Kachina." He is sometimes called Long Hair Kachina. If white feathers are hanging down on his black beard, he is called Downy Feathers Hanging Kachina. There is another, similar Kachina, called Santo Domingo Kokokshi. This Kachina has a red beard, so he is called the Red Beard Kachina.

Downy Feathers Hanging Kachina

Downy Feathers Hanging Kachina is a variation of the Kokokshi and is sometimes substituted for Kokokshi. As far as I know, Frank Vacit, Roger Cellicion (Bell, 1975, p. 13) and Andrea Lonjose Shirley have made this Kachina in jewelry.

Frank Vacit made this Downy Feathers Hanging Kachina bolo in the silver overlay/mosaic inlay style in the 1980s-1990s. It has his hallmark, F. VACIT-ZUNI, and his "ear of corn" hallmark. There is a colorful band between the blue face and the beard with hanging white feathers. There are stamped borders on both sides of the bolo slide. This stamp is frequently used by him. It measures 2.18 inches tall and consists of blue turquoise, red coral, white mother-of-pearl, gold lip mother-of-pearl, and black jet.

Silver overlay/mosaic inlay Downy Feathers Hanging Kachina bolo, Frank Vacit, F. VACIT-ZUNI & "ear of corn," 1980s-1990s, 1.94" x 2.18", $1000-1500.

This Downy Feathers Hanging Kachina bolo was made by Andrea Lonjose Shirley in the mosaic inlay style in 2003. He has a gourd in his right hand and a white fir branch in his left hand and stands still. Her lapidary is perfectly done. He seems to be a slim dancer. It measures 3.48 inches tall and consists of blue turquoise, red coral, white mother-of-pearl, gold lip mother-of-pearl, and black jet.

Mosaic inlay Downy Feathers Hanging Kachina bolo, Andrea Lonjose, ALS, 2003, 1.59" x 3.48", $300-450.

Kokokshi

Kokokshi, the long Hair Kachina, is the most sacred and powerful rain-making Kachina. In the Kokokshi dance, there are many Kokokshi Kachinas dancing in line, accompanied by a few Kachina Girls and other Kachinas.

Leonard Martza made this Kokokshi ring in the mosaic overlay style in 2009. I visited Leonard Martza at his house and asked him to make me some Kachina jewelry. Several days later, he completed this ring for me. The Kokokshi figure is made with blue turquoise, red spiny oyster, olive shell, and black jet with the background of white mother-of-pearl. He has a red band between the blue face and the black beard. As Kokokshi has black-and-white band, the artist might modify this part to avoid a violation of the taboo. It is a beautiful art work. The ring face measures 1.31 inches tall.

Mosaic overlay Long Hair Kachina ring, Leonard Martza, no hallmark, 2009, 0.72" x 1.31", $100-150.

This Kokokshi bolo was made by Leonard Martza in the mosaic overlay style in 2010. I asked him again to make me some Kachina jewelry on the next occasion. He made this Kokokshi figure. The figure consists of blue turquoise, red coral, orange spiny oyster, white mother-of-pearl, pink mother-of-pearl, and black jet. The band is the colorful one that Downy Feathers Hanging Kachina usually has. He has a gourd in his right hand. It measures 3.10 inches tall. It is a special piece of jewelry. Leonard Martza should be evaluated much more highly in the Zuni jewelry history.

Mosaic overlay Long Hair Kachina bolo, Leonard Martza, no hallmark, 2010, 2.23" x 3.10", $400-600.

Eldred Martinez made this Kokokshi pin in the mosaic inlay style in the 1990s. There are etchings all over the figure. This use of etchings is characteristic to Eldred. The form of stamps on silver drops is also unique to him. The figure faces to the left and raises his right knee slightly. It measures 1.96 inches tall and consists of blue/green turquoise, red and pink coral, white mother-of-pearl, and black jet.

Mosaic inlay Long Hair Kachina pin, Eldred Martinez, no hallmark, 1990s, 1.10" x 1.96", $80-120.

Kachinas in Other Ceremonies

There are other Kachinas so rarely made that they cannot be introduced with the other groups.

This Butterfly Kachina bolo was made by an unknown artist in the mosaic inlay style in the 1940s-1950s. As the face looks like a mask, it is not Tablita Maiden but Butterfly Kachina. One informant attributed this bolo to Myra Tucson, while another informant attributed it to one from the older generation of the Beyukas. Whoever made it, this bolo should be considered one of the best Zuni mosaic pieces of jewelry ever made. It measures 2.81 inches tall and consists of green turquoise, red spiny oyster, white mother-of-pearl, and black jet. This artist made this beautiful bolo using only four basic colors.

Mosaic inlay Butterfly Kachina bolo, artist unknown, no hallmark, 1940s-1950s, 1.83" x 2.81", $2000-3000.

This Hehe'a bolo was made by an unknown artist in the mosaic inlay style in the 1950s-1960s. The Hehe'a, or The Blunderer, Kachina, is sometimes called Candy Cane Kachina because of his red-and-white nose. He appears in the Corn Grinding ceremony as a helper for the corn grinding girls. One informant attributed it to Leo Poblano while another informant attributed it to Edward Beyuka. I am not certain about these attributions. This Kachina bolo is a rare but seemingly medium-grade piece of jewelry. It measures 3.23 inches tall and consists of green turquoise, red coral white mother-of-pearl, and brown pen shell.

Mosaic inlay Hehe'a bolo, artist unknown, no hallmark, 1950s-1960s, 1.69" x 3.23", $600-900.

Eldred Martinez made this Harvest Dancer pin in the mosaic inlay style in the late 1990s. This Kachina has corn in her right hand while raising the hand and right knee. There are many etchings all over the stones and shells and a lot of stamped silver drops. There are two types of stamped silver drops: one round and other oblong. It measures 3.68 inches tall and consists of blue turquoise, red coral, white mother-of-pearl, gold lip mother-of-pearl, synthesized opal, and black jet.

Mosaic inlay Harvest Dancer pin, Eldred Martinez, E Maltinez Zuni NM, 1990s, 1.80" x 3.68", $240-360.

Fabian Homer made this Kolowisi bolo in the mosaic overlay on spiny oyster style in 2010. This Kolowisi jewelry has been made by the Homers for years. Fabian's grandfather, Lambert Homer, Sr., made a Water Serpent pin/pendant in 1942 (Sotheby Park Bernet Inc., 1975, lot191), and his father, Lambert Homer, Jr., made a Sea Serpent or Kolowisi bolo in 1985 (Bassman, 1996, 35). They are all overlaid on the spiny oyster shell. Fabian Homer continues their legacy. Kolowisi appears in the initiation ceremony of younger children into the Kachina group and resides in the Zuni altars. It measures 3.45 inches tall and consists of blue turquoise, brown pen shell, white mother-of-pearl, and black jet.

Mosaic overlay on spiny oyster shell Kolowisi bolo, Fabian Homer, F Homer Zuni, 2010, 3.29" x 3.45", $400-600.

Edward Beyuka made this A:doshule Kachina bolo in the mosaic inlay style in the 1980s-1990s. This horrible Kachina appears in the Ground-Cleansing ceremony. He puts bad children in the basket he has on his back, and carries them away. He carries a knife in his right hand. In this bolo, a Mud Head kid is in the basket. It measures 4.66 inches tall and consists of blue turquoise, red coral, white mother-of-pearl, gold lip mother-of-pearl, yellow melon shell, iridescent abalone, dark brown pen shell, and black jet.

Mosaic inlay A:doshule bolo, Edward Beyuka, EAB, 1980s-1990s, 2.40" x 4.66", $1000-1500.

This Greasy Boys buckle, made by Frank Vavcit in the silver overlay and mosaic inlay style in the 1950s-1960s, is part of a men's set, along with the following bolo and watch bracelet. It is almost identical with the buckle in the *Arizona Highways* Hall of Fame collections. While mine is in the silver overlay and mosaic inlay style, the one from the collection seems to be made in the mosaic inlay in channels style. When I visited a museum gallery, I found this set in a show case. The manager asked me a lot about attributions of many older Zuni pieces and then gave me a discount for this set. We then talked about the attributions of older Zuni Knifewing and Rainbow Man pieces again for a while. At the last moment she told me she would ask the owner of this set for further discount. A few days later, she showed me a deeply discounted price, and I decided to get it. The boy seems to wear a rabbit fur around his neck and three eagle feathers on top of his head and from his ears. It measures 1.95 inches tall and consists of blue turquoise, red coral, brown cowrie shell, white mother-of-pearl, and black jet.

Mosaic inlay Greasy Boys buckle, Frank Vacit, ear of corn, 1950s-1960s, 2.99" x 1.95", $2000-3000.

Frank Vacit made a matching Greasy Boy bolo in the silver overlay and mosaic inlay style in the 1950s-1960s. It measures 2.02 inches tall and consists of blue turquoise, red coral, brown cowrie shell, white mother-of-pearl, and black jet.

Mosaic inlay Greasy Boys bolo, Frank Vacit, ear of corn, 1950s-1960s, 1.85" x 2.02", $2000-3000.

The matching Greasy Boy watch bracelet was also made by Frank Vacit in the silver overlay and mosaic inlay style in the 1950s-1960s. The watch tip measures 1.75 inches tall and consists of blue turquoise, red coral, brown cowrie shell, white mother-of-pearl, and black jet. They all have Vacit's "ear of corn" hallmark.

Mosaic inlay Greasy Boys watch bracelet, Frank Vacit, no hallmark, 1950s-1960s, 1.21" x 1.75", $2000-3000.

This Greasy Boys Kachina bolo was made by Edward Beyuka in the mosaic inlay style in the 1980s-1990s. These Kachinas appear in the Mixed Dance, carrying one another, but they dance one by one. It measures 5.14 inches tall and consists of blue turquoise, red coral, white mother-of-pearl, iridescent abalone, brown pen shell, and black jet.

Mosaic inlay Greasy Boys bolo, Edward Beyuka, EAB, 1980s-1990s, 2.75" x 5.14", $1000-1500.

V.
Dancers in the Social Dances

There are other dances performed in Zuni that have less religious significance. They are performed for the joy of the performers and the pleasure for the spectators. In these dances, performers usually dance without masks on their faces.

There are Eagle Dancers, Comanche Dancers, Buffalo Dancers, Hoop Dancers, Paw Wow Dancers, and Olla or Pottery Dancers.

Eagle Dancers

The Eagle Dancer has been made in jewelry in quantity by various artists. He wears an eagle cap instead of the eagle mask worn by the Eagle Kachina. Consequently, you can see the eagle Dancer's expression clearly. You can easily differentiate the Eagle Kachina from the Eagle Dancer by this difference.

Ted Edaakie made this Eagle Dancer bolo in the mosaic inlay style in 1940s-1950s. Please refer to the Eagle Dancer pin from the *The C. G. Wallace Collection of American Indian Art* auction catalog (Sotheby Park Bernet Inc., 1975, pp. 54-55). Although the number and the content of the caption do not match, the central Eagle Dancer was clearly made by Ted Edaakie in 1942. The number of the picture should be 285. Please look at the Sun Face in his kilt and the stop motion posture during dancing. He bends his knees slightly and extends his wings widely. In addition, a colorful sash hangs down from his waist. All of these aspects enhance the attractiveness of this Eagle Dancer. In my opinion, this should be a representative example of the Eagle Dancer design. It measures 3.78 inches tall and consists of blue turquoise, red/orange spiny oyster, iridescent abalone, white mother-of-pearl, and black jet.

Mosaic inlay Eagle Dancer bolo, Theodore Edaakie, no hallmark, 1940s-1950s, 3.69" x 3.78", $1200-1800.

This Eagle dancer bolo was made by Ted Edaakie in the mosaic inlay style in the 1940s-1950s. This Eagle Dancer raises his right leg higher than the previous dancer and extends his wings narrower downwards. A colorful sash flies high in the air, and a sun face decorates his kilt. The blue turquoise part under his face is more complex than the one from the previous Eagle Dancer bolo. There are two colorful matching bolo tips of eagle feathers, enhancing this bolo's attractiveness. It measures 3.89 inches tall and consists of blue turquoise, orange spiny oyster, white mother-of-pearl, iridescent abalone, and black jet.

Mosaic inlay Eagle Dancer bolo, Theodore Edaakie, no hallmark, 1940s-1950s, 3.96" x 3.89", $1200-1800.

An Eagle Dancer bolo probably made in the mosaic inlay style in the 1940s-1950s. The dancer stands still and sets his face straight forward. The bolo has matching bolo tips of the dancer's feet. It measures 2.97 inches tall and consists of blue turquoise, orange spiny oyster, white mother-of-pearl, iridescent abalone, and black jet.

Mosaic inlay Eagle Dancer bolo, Theodore Edaakie?, no hallmark, 1940s-1950s, 2.43" x 2.97", $600-900.

This Eagle Dancer bolo, made by an unknown artist in the mosaic inlay style in the 1940s-1950s, has simple Hopi birds for its bolo tips. He slightly bends his knees and extends his wings. It is a simple but cute Eagle Dancer figure. One informant attributed it to John Lucio, but I am not sure about the attribution. It measures 2.57 inches tall and consists of blue turquoise, orange spiny oyster, white mother-of-pearl, and black jet.

Mosaic inlay Eagle Dancer bolo, artist unknown, no hallmark, 1940s-1950s, 2.06" x 2.57", $400-600.

This Eagle Dancer bolo was probably made by John Lucio in the mosaic inlay style in the 1950s-1960s. This Eagle Dancer extends his wings widely downwards, while the stepping motion is not apparent, making him look static. This design reminds me of the work of Larry Laiwaate in the 1980s. It measures 2.57 inches tall and consists of blue/green turquoise, red spiny oyster, white mother-of-pearl, black jet, and tortoise shell.

Mosaic inlay Eagle Dancer bolo, John Lucio?, no hallmark, 1950s-1960s, 2.58" x 2.57", $400-600.

John Lucio made this Eagle Dancer bolo in the mosaic inlay style in the 1960s-1970s. The dancer extends his wings widely downwards. While his stepping motion is not apparent, slight movement in his right legs can be observed. Red-and-black end of his sash belt hangs down clearly from his left waist. The figure measures 2.69 inches tall and consists of blue turquoise, red coral, white mother-of-pearl, and black jet.

Mosaic inlay Eagle Dancer bolo, John Lucio?, no hallmark, 1950s-1960s, 2.26" x 2.69", $400-600.

This Eagle Dancer bolo was also made by John Lucio in the mosaic inlay style in the 1970s-1980s. This is his famous standard Eagle Dancer design. The eagle cap, turquoise parts on his wings, and white moccasin covers are set slightly higher, and the silverwork of twisted wires and stamped silver drops is evident. These twisted silver wires might be a plain symbol of snakes. The bolo slide measures 1.87 inches tall and consists of blue turquoise, red coral, white mother-of-pearl, and black jet.

Mosaic inlay Eagle Dancer bolo, John Lucio, J LUCIO, 1960s-1970s, 1.88" x 1.87", $400-600.

A matching Eagle Dancer buckle was made by John Lucio in the mosaic inlay style in the 1970s-1980s. The eagle cap, turquoise parts in his wings, and white moccasin covers are set slightly higher, and the gorgeous silverwork of snakes and the stamped silver drops enhance the attractiveness of this buckle. The Eagle Dancer figure measures 2.25 inches tall, and the buckle measures 3.44 inches tall. It consists of blue turquoise, red coral, white mother-of-pearl, and black jet.

Mosaic inlay Eagle Dancer buckle, John Lucio, J LUCIO, 1950s-1960s, 2.72" x 3.44", $600-900.

This Eagle Dancer bolo was probably made by Dixon Shebola in the mosaic inlay style in the 1950s-1960s. An online gallery attributes an almost identical one to Dennis Edaakie, while my informants attribute it variously to Oliver Cellicion, Dexter Cellicion, John Lucio, Edward Beyuka or Lambert Homer. Finally, an informant who is a brother of Dixon Shebola confirmed it as Dixon's work. This Eagle Dancer faces his body straight forward, while raising his right knee high; his head turns to his right. All parts are set flat in the channels except for the blue and red necklace. It measures 2.65 inches tall and consists of blue turquoise, red coral, white mother-of-pearl, and black jet.

Mosaic inlay Eagle Dancer bolo, Dixon Shebola, no hallmark, 1950s-1960s, 2.77" x 2.65", $1000-1500.

This is an Eagle Dancer bolo probably made by Dixon Shebola in the mosaic inlay style in the 1960s-1970s. Although it is made almost identically to the bolo described just above, the kilt pattern is more complex and the necklace is made solely with turquoise. It measures 3.38 inches tall and consists of blue turquoise, red coral, white mother-of-pearl, and black jet.

Mosaic inlay Eagle Dancer bolo, Dixon Shebola, no hallmark, 1960s-1970, 3.40" x 3.38", $1000-1500.

Dixon Shebola made this Eagle Dancer buckle in the mosaic inlay style in the 1960s-1970s. The head and the eye of this figure are round. This feature may make the figure look younger. Except for this point, this figure is identical with the bolos just described. Four snake eye turquoise cabochons are set in the four corners of the buckle, and the outer edges are stamped heavily. The figure and buckle measure 1.96 and 2.30 inches tall respectively. The figure consists of blue turquoise, red coral, white mother-of-pearl, and black jet.

Mosaic inlay Eagle Dancer buckle, Dixon Shebola, no hallmark, 1960s-1970, 3.03" x 2.30", $1000-1500.

This Eagle Dancer bolo was made by Charlie and Mary Ann Poncho in the mosaic inlay style in the 1960s. It has eaglets for bolo tips. An eaglet has a round eye, while the eagle has a rectangular eye. The necklace, pendant, and feathers of these three figures are set slightly higher than the bodies. The eye of the eagle is set upside down. This setting makes the eyesight of this Eagle Dancer keener. The bolo slide has a smaller "CMP ZUNI" hallmark on its back while the eaglets of the bolo tips have larger "C. M. P. ZUNI NM" hallmarks on their backs. The Ponchos used the two types of their hallmarks interchangeably in the 1960s. The Dancer raises his right knee slightly and turns his face to his right. It measures 3.45 inches tall and consists of blue turquoise, red coral, white mother-of-pearl, gold lip mother-of-pearl, iridescent abalone, dark brown pen shell, and black jet.

Mosaic inlay Eagle Dancer bolo, Charles and Mary Ann Poncho, CMP ZUNI, 1960s, 3.33" x 3.45", $600-900.

Charlie and Mary Ann Poncho made this Eagle Dancer bolo in the mosaic inlay style in the 1970s-1980s. It has eaglets for bolo tips as well. The eye setting of the Eagle Dancer is different from the setting of the bolo just described and is the same as that of their bolo in *Zuni: the Art and the People* (Bell, 1975, 37). It measures 3.51 inches tall and consists of blue turquoise, red coral, white mother-of-pearl, gold lip mother-of-pearl, iridescent abalone, dark brown pen shell, and black jet.

Mosaic inlay Eagle Dancer bolo, Charles and Mary Ann Poncho, CMP ZUNI, 1970s-1980s, 3.29" x 3.51", $600-900.

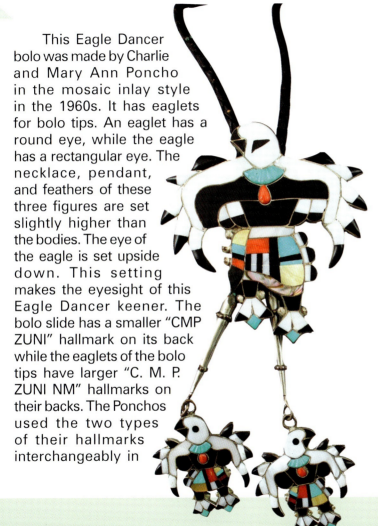

This Eagle Dancer pin/pendant was made by Charlie and Mary Ann Poncho in the mosaic inlay style in the 1950s-1960s. It has no hallmark on its back. As they began making jewelry in the early 1950s, it is not surprising that the works were released without inscription. The partly raised inlay work and the eye setting are same with the bolo made in the 1970s. The Dancer measures 2.29 inches tall and the round pin/pendant measures 2.61 inches in diameter. It consists of blue turquoise, red coral, white mother-of-pearl, gold lip mother-of-pearl, iridescent abalone, and black jet.

Mosaic inlay Eagle Dancer pin/pendant, Charles and Mary Ann Poncho, no hallmark, 1950s-1960s, 2.61" across, $200-300.

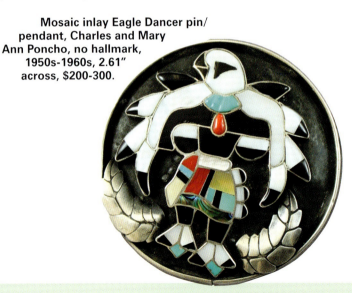

Charlie and Mary Ann Poncho made this Eagle Dancer ring in the mosaic inlay style in the 1970s-1980s. This ring has a smaller "CMP ZUNI" hallmark on its back. It measures 1.53 inches tall and consists of blue turquoise, red coral, white mother-of-pearl, gold lip mother-of-pearl, dark brown pen shell, and black jet.

Mosaic inlay Eagle Dancer ring, Charles and Mary Ann Poncho, CMP ZUNI, 1970s-1980s, 1.54" x 1.53", $100-150.

Edward Beyuka made this Eagle Dancer bolo in the mosaic inlay style in the 1950s. He depicts the Eagle Dancer showing its back while dancing, which is also sometimes depicted by great artists such as Bruce Zunie and Frank Vacit. Most artists depict the dancer in the frontal view. One end of this dancer's sash flies in the air, while another end hangs still from his waist. The tail of the Eagle Dancer on his back is extremely colorful and gorgeous. This might be an Eagle Dancer for the Pow Wow, because it is so colorful. He raises his right knee and extends his both hands widely. The bolo measures 3.40 inches tall and consists of blue turquoise, red coral, orange abalone, white mother-of-pearl, and black jet.

Mosaic inlay Eagle Dancer bolo, Edward Beyuka, no hallmark, 1950s, 2.75" x 3.40", $600-900.

This Eagle Dancer pin/ pendant was made by Edward Beyuka in the 1970s-1980s. The Dancer raises his right knee slightly; his head faces straight forward. The silver walls of the channels show different thicknesses, which is characteristic to his jewelry. Although the lapidary work is done solely with turquoise, some parts are carved and raised slightly higher than the body. It measures 2.36 inches tall, which is small for his pieces.

Mosaic inlay Eagle Dancer pin/ pendant, Edward Beyuka, EAB, 1970s-1980s, 1.94" x 2.36", $400-600.

Madeline Beyuka made this Eagle Dancer pin/pendant in the mosaic inlay style in the 1970s-1990s. This design is the same as the one used by her former husband, Edward Beyuka, although her dancer stands still, and carved and plain turquoise parts are set flush. It measures 1.99 inches tall.

Mosaic inlay Eagle Dancer pin/pendant, Madeline Beyuka, MB, 1970s-1990s, 1.51" x 1.99", $200-300.

These Eagle Dancer earrings were made by Madeline Beyuka in the mosaic inlay style in the 1970s-1990s. They match the pendant introduced above very well. Each earring measures 1.54 inches tall. Both earrings have vertically stamped "MB" hallmarks on their backs.

Mosaic inlay Eagle Dancer earrings, Madeline Beyuka, MB, 1970s-1990s, 1.12" x 1.54", $200-300.

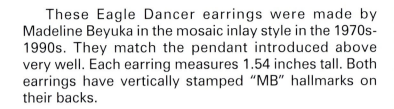

This Eagle Dancer bolo was made by an unknown artist in the mosaic inlay style in the 1940s-1950s. Although its size is very small (1.13 inches tall), all its parts are carved in the cubic manner, which is an older mosaic inlay style. Look at the face and head. A tiny white part is inlaid in the white eagle cap. An informant has attributed it to Edward Beyuka, while his ex-wife, Madeline Beyuka, refutes the attribution. It consists of blue turquoise, orange spiny oyster, white mother-of-pearl, and black jet.

Mosaic inlay Eagle Dancer bolo, artist unknown, no hallmark, 1940s-1950s, 1.82" x 1.13", $200-300.

Helen and Lincoln Zunie made this Eagle Dancer buckle in mosaic inlay style in the 1970s-1980s. The Eagle Dancer is set in the octagonal background, made with gold lip mother-of-pearl, and the four corners of the buckle are set with blue turquoise. The Eagle Dancer faces to his right and dances while raising his right knee slightly and extending his right hand upward and his left hand downward. The figure consists of blue turquoise, red coral, white mother-of-pearl, iridescent abalone, black jet, and yellow aluminum.

Mosaic inlay Eagle Dancer buckle, Helen Lincoln Zunie, H-L. ZUNIE, 1970s-1980s, 3.52" x 2.36", $500-750.

This Eagle Dancer bolo was made by William and Geneva Zunie in the mosaic inlay style in the 1960s-1980s. Its posture looks as if he is jumping, bending both knees upward. It measures 1.97 inches tall and consists of blue turquoise, red coral, white mother-of-pearl, iridescent abalone, and black jet.

Mosaic inlay Eagle Dancer bolo, William and Geneva Zunie, WM. ZUNIE, 1960s-1980s, 1.50" x 1.97", $120-180.

William and Geneva Zunie made this Eagle Dancer pin in the mosaic inlay style in the 1960s-1980s. The posture is just like the bolo slide described above. It measures 2.03 inches tall and consists of blue turquoise, red coral, white mother-of-pearl, iridescent abalone, and black jet.

Mosaic inlay Eagle Dancer pin, William and Geneva Zunie, no hallmark, 1960s-1980s, 1.68" x 2.03", $120-180.

Comanche Dancer

According to my informant, if a dancer puts on a full feathered bonnet, he is a Comanche Kachina or Comanche Dancer. If his face looks like a mask, he should be a Comanche Kachina. If he wears no mask, he should be a Comanche Dancer, one of the Social Dancers like the Eagle Dancer. If a Dancer wears a few feathers over the top of his head, he could be an Apache Kachina or Dancer.

This Comanche Dancer bolo was made by Cecilia and John Lucio in the mosaic inlay style in the 1940s-1950s. His face is three-dimensionally carved, and the eyes are carved in and dyed with black pigment. The bonnet, hair, and necklace are made with the flush inlay technique. It measures 2.21 inches tall and consists of green turquoise, red coral, white mother-of-pearl, and black jet.

Mosaic inlay Comanche Dancer bolo, Cecilia and John Lucio, no hallmark, 1940s-1950s, 2.57" x 2.21", $1200-1800.

Cecilia and John Lucio made this Comanche Dancer bolo in the mosaic inlay style in the 1940s-1950s. It is a smaller bolo slide (1.47 inches tall), but it is made in exactly the same manner as the larger bolo described just above. My informant told me this was Cecilia's older piece. It consists of blue turquoise, red coral, white mother-of-pearl, and black jet. Its bolo clasps are made with two silver plates instead of silver wires.

Mosaic inlay Comanche Dancer bolo, Cecilia and John Lucio, no hallmark, 1940s-1950s, 1.57" x 1.47", $400-600.

This Comanche Dancer bolo was made by Cecilia and John Lucio in the mosaic inlay style in the 1940s-1950s. An online article attributed an almost identical piece to Teddy Weahkee. The face of this bolo is also three-dimensionally carved, and black pigment is put in all of the recessed areas of the face. The feathered bonnet, hair ornaments, and necklace are made in the flush inlay style. The bonnet looks very colorful because of its red and white colors, compared with the bolo just described. Its bolo clasps are made with two round and one W-shaped silver wires. This bolo measures 1.55 inches tall and consists of blue/green turquoise, red coral, white mother-of-pearl, iridescent abalone, and black jet.

Mosaic inlay Comanche Dancer bolo, Cecilia and John Lucio, no hallmark, 1940s-1950s, 1.66" x 1.55", $400-600.

This Comanche Dancer bolo, made by Cecilia and John Lucio in the mosaic inlay style in the 1940s-1950s, is made in exactly the same manner with the bolo described at the left, except that the black pigment is not put along its raised nose. It measures 1.63 inches tall and consists of blue/green turquoise, red coral, white mother-of-pearl, iridescent abalone, and black jet. Its bolo clasps are also identical with the bolo clasps of the above-presented bolo.

Mosaic inlay Comanche Dancer bolo, Cecilia and John Lucio, no hallmark, 1940s-1950s, 1.69" x 1.63", $400-600.

Another Comanche Dancer bolo, by Cecilia and John Lucio in the mosaic inlay style in the 1940s-1950s, is made in exactly the same manner with the bolo described on the previous page, including its bolo clasps. It is the smallest of the four at 1.47 inches tall. It consists of blue/green turquoise, red coral, white mother-of-pearl, iridescent abalone, and black jet.

Mosaic inlay Comanche Dancer bolo, Cecilia and John Lucio, no hallmark, 1940s-1950s, 1.61" x 1.47", $400-600.

This Comanche Dancer bolo was made by an unknown artist in the mosaic inlay style in the 1950s-1960s. All shell and stone parts are set higher than the top of silver channels. One informant attributed it to Leo Poblano, while another one attributed to Dexter Cellicion. I personally think that it might be made by Leo Poblano's brother, Sam Poblano, because of its facial expression. It measures 2.90 inches tall and consists of blue turquoise, orange spiny oyster, white mother-of-pearl, gold lip mother-of-pearl, yellow melon shell, black mother-of-pearl, and black jet.

Mosaic inlay Comanche Dancer bolo, artist unknown, no hallmark, 1950s-1960s, 3.23" x 2.90", $500-750.

A Comanche Dancer bolo made by Ralph Quam in the mosaic inlay style in the 1970s-1980s. Ralph's wife told to Ernie Bulow that this design has been made much less than the one in profile. It is very similar to the Comanche Dancer bolo described just above. This bolo has thinner face and fewer eagle feathers, and its facial expression is bolder and not so perfect, according to his wife. It measures 2.5 inches tall and consists of blue turquoise, orange spiny oyster, white mother-of-pearl and dark brown pen shell.

Mosaic inlay Comanche Dancer bolo, Ralph Quam, R. Quam, 1960s-1980s, 2.5" x 2.5", $400-600.

This Comanche Dancer bolo was probably made by Ralph Quam in the mosaic inlay style in the 1960s-1970s. Ten small dots are inlaid inside the end of feather and head band. This dot inlay enhances the attractiveness of this bolo slide. A hand written hallmark of "R. Q." is scratched on the back. It measures 1.79 inches tall and consists of blue/green turquoise, orange spiny oyster, yellow fossilized walrus ivory, white mother-of-pearl, black mother-of-pearl, and dark brown pen shell.

Mosaic inlay Comanche Dancer bolo, Ralph Quam, R.Q., 1960s-1970s, 1.72" x 1.79", $300-450.

Corida and Quincy Peynetsa made this Comanche Dancer bolo in the silver overlay and mosaic inlay style in the 1950s-1960s. The lapidary work is almost identical with the five Comanche Dancer bolos made by Cecilia and John Lucio. Technically this bolo slide is made very well, but I think it is not good enough artistically because it is not their original design. It measures 2.01 inches in diameter and consists of blue turquoise, red coral, white mother-of-pearl, and black jet.

Silver overlay/mosaic inlay Comanche Dancer bolo, Corida and Quincy Peynetsa, no hallmark, 1950s-1960s, 2.01" across, $200-300.

111

This Comanche Dancer bolo was probably made by Mary Ann Cellicion alone (without Dexter Cellicion) in the mosaic overlay style in the 1940s-1950s. The eye, eyebrow, and mouth are slightly carved. The two matching bolo tips enhance its attractiveness. The bolo slide and bolo tips measure 2.06 and 1.32 inches tall, respectively. They consist of blue/green turquoise, orange spiny oyster, white mother-of-pearl, and black jet.

Mosaic overlay Comanche Dancer bolo, Mary Ann Cellicion?, no hallmark, 1940s-1950s, 1.28" x 2.06", $400-600.

Mary Ann Cellicion is probably also the maker of this Comanche Dancer buckle in the mosaic overlay style in the 1940s-1950s. Although the designs of the bolo above and the buckle are slightly different, they were probably made by the same artist. There are four rectangular turquoise stones set on the four corners of the silver buckle, and a lot of X-shaped stamps are put all over the frame. While the four corners within the frame are stamped with two kinds of dies, the remaining area is left unstamped. The buckle and the figure measure 2.45 and 1.90 inches tall, respectively. The figure consists of blue turquoise, orange spiny oyster, white mother-of-pearl, and black jet.

Mosaic overlay Comanche Dancer buckle, Mary Ann Cellicion?, no hallmark, 1940s-1950s, 3.55" x 2.45", $400-600.

Edward Beyuka made this Comanche Dancer bolo in the mosaic inlay style in the 1980s. The Dancer raises his right knee high and has a tomahawk in his right hand. The eye, nose, and mouth are carved with precision, and stamped silver waist and head bands are set effectively to enhance his attractiveness. The bolo tips are carved eagle feathers. Beyuka does not frequently use this design for his bolo tips. It measures 4.89 inches tall and consists of blue turquoise, red coral, white mother-of-pearl, black mother-of-pearl, yellow fossilized walrus ivory, and black jet.

Mosaic inlay Comanche Dancer bolo, Edward Beyuka, EAB ZUNI, 1980s, 2.92" x 4.89", $1000-1500.

This is a Comanche Drummer bolo made by Edward Beyuka in the mosaic inlay style in the 1970s-1980s. The eye, nose, and mouth are carved, and a pigment is put in them so that his facial expression becomes clearer. He raises his right knee high as if he is dancing. It measures 5.93 inches tall and consists of blue turquoise, red coral, white mother-of-pearl, iridescent abalone, yellow fossilized walrus ivory, and black jet.

Mosaic inlay Comanche Drummer bolo, Edward Beyuka, EAB ZUNI, 1970s-1980s, 3.13" x 5.93", $1200-1800.

Dixon Shebola made this Comanche Dancer bolo made by in the mosaic inlay style in the 1950s-1960s. It is signed "-shebala-," using an electric pen. It is an extraordinarily huge bolo (6.87 inches tall). Shebola made a silver backing first with a detailed channels and welded silver balls alongside both legs. These balls may represent silver bells; they ring when a dancer steps fiercely. Then Shebola sets various colorful stones and shells with a lot of carvings in those channels. Some parts are set slightly higher than the rest, giving this bolo a three dimensional effect. The special feature of this piece is that the flower-like ornament on his right elbow is removable and can be used as a tie pin. The pin is set securely on the bolo by using male and female screws. His war bonnet has two buffalo horns, and a lot of eagle feathers are set on his lower back. He has a tomahawk in his right hand and raises his left knee higher. It consists of blue turquoise, red coral, yellow olive shell, white mother-of-pearl, yellow and brown tortoise shell, and black jet. In addition, silver is used for the main part of the tomahawk.

Mosaic inlay Comanche Dancer bolo, Dixon Shebola, -shebala-, 1970s-1980s, 3.88" x 6.87", $1600-2400.

Buffalo Dancer

The Buffalo Dance is performed in the various pueblos along the Rio Grande River and introduced in Zuni as a Social Dance. Zuni has a Buffalo Kachina as well. He wears a full mask which looks like a real Buffalo. A Buffalo Dancer in a Social Dance wears a buffalo cap so that performer's face can be clearly seen.

This Buffalo Dancer bolo was made by an unknown artist in the mosaic inlay style in the 1940s-1950s. The bolo has smaller Buffalo Dancer heads for its bolo tips. The dancer wears a kilt with a serpent on it. He has a gourd in his right hand and a bow in his left hand. He also bends his right knee slightly. This posture makes us feel movement of the dancer. Concerning its artist, one informant attributed it to Leo Poblano, while another informant attributed it to John Lucio. There might be still other possibilities. It measures 3.47 inches tall and consists of blue turquoise, red abalone, white clam shell, iridescent abalone, brown and yellow tortoise shell, black jet, and unknown yellow stone or shell.

Mosaic inlay Buffalo Dancer bolo, artist unknown, no hallmark, 1940s-1950s, 1.58" x 3.47", $1000-1500.

John Lucio made this Buffalo Dancer bolo in the mosaic inlay style in the 1940s-1950s. His face is all black and carved to make his nose slightly higher and his mouth a little lower. Two smaller eyes are inlaid with white dots. This facial carving is the same as that of John's Hopi Snake Dancer described in the next chapter. The Dancer raises his both hands high in the air, holding a gourd in his right hand and a bow in his left hand. A red-and-blue wavy band in his kilt might depict a snake. The thin arms and legs and moccasins with white covers are characteristic of various figures made by John. It measures 3.28 inches tall and consists of blue/green turquoise, red spiny oyster, white clam shell, yellow and brown tortoise shell, iridescent abalone, dark brown pen shell, and black jet.

Mosaic inlay Buffalo Dancer bolo, John Lucio, no hallmark, 1940s-1950s, 2.09" x 3.28", $1000-1500.

This Buffalo Dancer bolo was made by John Lucio in the mosaic inlay style in the 1950s-1960s. The dancer's upper face is black and his lower face is white. The upper half is carved to make his nose slightly higher, and two white dots are inlaid in it. There is no mouth carved in his lower face. He raises both hands high while holding a gourd in his right hand and a bow in his left hand. There is no wavy band of snake on his kilt, but there is a sash hanging down from his waist. There are a lot of small stamped silver drops all around his body. This stamp is identical with those of his hallmarked Eagle Dancer pieces. Consequently, we can safely say this and the previous Buffalo Dancers were made by John Lucio. It measures 3.09 inches tall and consists of blue/green turquoise, red coral, white mother-of-pearl, brown and yellow tortoise shell, dark brown pen shell, and black jet.

Mosaic inlay Buffalo Dancer bolo, John Lucio, no hallmark, 1950s-1960s, 2.56" x 3.98", $1000-1500.

This Buffalo Dancer bolo was made by John Lucio in the mosaic inlay style in the 1940s-1950s. This bolo might be made earlier than two bolos described above because those bolos resemble closely with each other, and their moccasin covers are apparently different from the one on this bolo. Since one of the more complex bolos was made in the 1950s-1960s, this simpler piece may be older. This bolo has matching smaller Buffalo Dancers for bolo tips which measure 1.47 inches tall. The upper half of the face is black, while the lower half is white, and the nose is carved slightly higher. The eyes are inlaid with small white dots. The dancer raises both hands high, having a gourd in his right hand and a bow in his left hand. His right knee is slightly raised. The colorful sash is around his waist from where its end hangs. It measures 3.98 inches tall and consists of blue turquoise, red spiny oyster, white mother-of-pearl, yellow and brown tortoise shell, dark brown pen shell, and black jet.

Mosaic inlay Buffalo Dancer bolo, John Lucio, no hallmark, 1940s-1950s, 2.53" x 3.99", $1000-1500.

Edward Beyuka made this Buffalo Dancer bolo in the mosaic inlay style in 2001. The dancer raises his right knee slightly and has an eagle feather in his left hand. There are stamped silver platelets in his upper arms and around his waist. The hand-made silver drums signify this bolo being made by Beyuka. It measures 4.87 inches tall and consists of blue turquoise, red coral, white mother-of-pearl, gold lip mother-of-pearl, dark brown pen shell, and black jet.

Mosaic inlay Buffalo Dancer bolo, Edward Beyuka, EAB ZUNI, 2001, 2.57" x 4.87", $1000-1500.

This Buffalo Dancer bracelet with the lapidary work was done by Anna Rita and Lambert Homer, Jr., in the mosaic inlay in mother-of-pearl style in the 1970s-1980s. Although there is no hallmark, it is confirmed as their work by Anna Rita Homer. The dancer stands still while holding a gourd in his right hand and a stick or bow in his left hand. The almost identical Buffalo ring is featured in *Zuni Jewelry* (Bassman, 1992, p. 16). The Bassmans attributed it to Delfina Cachini. However, an online seller told me that its lapidary work was done by Anna Rita and Lambert Homer, Jr., while the cluster work was done by Delfine Nastacio. The medallion measures 2.01 inches tall and consists of blue turquoise, red coral, white mother-of-pearl, and black jet.

Mosaic inlay Buffalo Dancer bracelet, Anna Rita and Lambert Homer Jr., no hallmark, 1970s-1980s, 1.93" x 2.40", $500-750.

The lapidary work on this Buffalo Dancer pin was done by Anna Rita and Lambert Homer Jr. in the mosaic inlay in mother-of-pearl style in the 1980s, and the silver work was done by Curtis Kucate in 2011. Lambert cut out the mother-of-pearl shell which is covered with aluminum for its back. Anna Rita then inlaid the figure in the recessed area. This insert was sold to a trader or silversmith, and it remained unset in silver. I acquired two of these unset inserts and asked my friend, Curtis Kucate, to set one of them in silver as a pin. It measures 2.26 inches tall and consists of blue turquoise, red coral, white mother-of-pearl, gold lip mother-of-pearl, and black jet.

Mosaic inlay Buffalo Dancer pin, lapidary work by Anna Rita and Lambert Homer Jr. and silver work by Curtis Kucate, no hallmark, 1980s and 2011 respectively, 1.74" x 2.26", $300-450.

This is a Buffalo Dancer bolo with lapidary work by Anna Rita and Lambert Homer, Jr., in the mosaic inlay in mother-of-pearl style in the 1980s, and the silver work by Curtis Kucate in 2011. It measures 2.25 inches tall and consists of blue turquoise, red coral, white mother-of-pearl, gold lip mother-of-pearl, and black jet.

Mosaic inlay Buffalo Dancer bolo, lapidary work by Anna Rita and Lambert Homer Jr. and silver work by Curtis Kucate, no hallmark, 1980s and 2011 respectively, 1.74" x 2.25", $300-450.

Olla Maiden

The Olla Maiden dance is very popular, and various Zuni Olla Maiden dance groups have toured all over the United States, including Young Pottery Maidens (Thelma Sheche and her successor and daughter, Lorandina Sheche, are in this group). A long time ago, Zuni ladies used to go to a well to fill a large water jar up with water and carried it home on their heads. This old custom was transformed first into a procession of Zuni ladies with water jars on their heads, and then into an Olla Maiden Dancer with a water pot on her head (Bulow, August 2012, pp. 20-22).

This Olla Maiden bracelet was made by Mabel Lonjose in the mosaic overlay style in the 1970s-1980s. The turquoise necklace and small silver drops are set on her chest. This is a rare technique. The maiden wears a traditional Manta dress and a white apron, and puts on a pair of white moccasins.

Her face, moccasins, and apron are carved, and black pigment is put in the recessed areas. Six silver drops along the lower right side of her dress might represent Manta pins, which fasten the open side of the Manta dress. The medallion measures 4.43 inches tall and consists of blue turquoise, red coral, white mother-of-pearl, and black jet.

Mosaic overlay Olla maiden bracelet, Mabel Lonjose, C/ MCL and an arrow, 1970s-1980s, 1.33" x 4.43", $600-900.

Mabel Lonjose made this Olla Maiden pin in the mosaic overlay style in the 1970s-1980s. It is made in exactly the same manner with the bracelet described just above. It measures 4.90 inches tall and consists of blue turquoise, red spiny oyster, white mother-of-pearl, and black jet.

Mosaic overlay Olla maiden pin, Mabel Lonjose, C/MCL and an arrow, 1970s-1980s, 1.37" x 4.90", $600-900.

This Olla Maiden ring was made by Jack Mahkee in the mosaic inlay style in the 1970s-1980s. She wears a traditional Manta Dress, back scarf, and moccasins. The four round blue dots might represent turquoise manta pins. It measures only 1.69 inches long, including the jar on her head. Considering this smaller size, this figure is uniquely and very complexly built. He should be considered a great artist. It consists of blue turquoise, white mother-of-pearl, yellow fossilized walrus ivory, black mother-of-pearl, and black jet.

Mosaic inlay Olla maiden ring, Jack Mahkee, J Mahkee, 1970s-1980s, 0.59" x 1.69", $100-150.

Madeline Beyuka made this Olla Maiden ring in the mosaic inlay style in the 1980s-1990s. This is her typical Olla Maiden design. The maiden is in the traditional formal Zuni dress with a colorful jar on her head. Her facial expression is well carved on her round face, and drape carvings of her sleeves make this figure realistic. This could be the best conceived and executed Olla Maiden design. It measures 2.26 inches tall and consists of blue turquoise, red coral, white mother-of-pearl, yellow fossilized walrus ivory, black jet, and a yellow metal.

Mosaic inlay Olla maiden ring, Madeline Beyuka, MB, 1980s-1990s, 1.02" x 2.26", $100-150.

This Olla Maiden ring was made by Madeline Beyuka in the mosaic inlay style in the 1950s-1960s. It may be among her earliest pieces. The maiden is in the formal Manta dress with a large water jar or Olla on her head. Her face is long and narrow, and the eyes and mouth are incised slightly. I have an almost identical Zuni lady ring without an Olla. This one measures 1.53 inches tall and consists of green turquoise, red coral, yellow olive shell, white mother-of-pearl, and black jet. Considering this smaller size, Madeline's lapidary skill is marvelous.

Mosaic inlay Olla maiden ring, Madeline Beyuka, no hallmark, 1950s-1960s, 0.48" x 1.53", $150-225.

Other Dancers

This section discusses the remaining Zuni Social Dancers. The length of the section is limited since I have been able to collect only one each.

Leo Poblano made this Tablita Dancer bolo in the mosaic inlay style in the late 1950s. The dancer's facial expression is carved in an expert manner that can be executed only by the greatest artist. The colorfully painted board is called Tablita and can be seen at the Pueblo Corn Dance frequently. The dancer raises his right knee slightly. He has an eagle feather in both of his hands, raising his left arm upward and putting his right hand downward. His kilt, sash, and a kind of shirt are colorfully executed. This could be a museum piece. It measures 4.16 inches tall and consists of blue/green turquoise, red spiny oyster, white mother-of-pearl, yellow fossilized walrus ivory, dark brown pen shell, and black jet.

Mosaic inlay Tablita Dancer bolo, Leo Poblano, no hallmark, 1950s, 2.31" x 4.16", $4000-6000.

This Hoop Dancer pin was made by John Lucio in the mosaic inlay style in the 1950s. This design is made by Edward Beyuka as well, but I have not been able to acquire it. In this pin, the dancer's hair is set slightly higher than the remaining body. His thin arms and legs and the silver work clearly show it to be John Lucio's work. The figure is dancing, raising his right knee high, with a silver hoop in each hand. It measures 2.64 inches tall and consists of blue turquoise, red spiny oyster, white mother-of-pearl, and black jet.

Mosaic inlay Hoop Dancer pin, John Lucio, no hallmark, 1950s, 1.92" x 2.64", $1000-1500.

This Female Dancer bolo was made by an unknown artist in the mosaic inlay style in the 1940s-1950s. One informant says she is a Corn Maiden, another says she is a Greasy boys' Mother, and a third informant says she is not a Kachina but a Maiden Dancer. One informant attributed it to Leo Poblano, while another informant attributed it to John Lucio. Whoever made it, this is an old-style of Kachina jewelry. The ornament around her face might be a Tablita. If so, she might be a Corn Dancer. It measures 2.94 inches tall and consists of green turquoise, red spiny oyster, white mother-of-pearl, yellow and brown tortoise shell, and black jet.

Mosaic inlay Maiden Dancer bolo, artist unknown, no hallmark, 1940s-1950s, 1.53" x 2.94", $1000-1500.

This Pow Wow Dancer bolo was made by an unknown artist in the channel inlay style in the 1950s-1960s. I bought it at the Tobe Turpen Indian Trading Company more than 10 years ago. This bolo has a label saying "1950's Edward Beyuka." However, Madeline Beyuka confidently denies that the piece is Edward's, and its style is not his famous one. It measures 2.97 inches tall and consists solely of turquoise.

Mosaic inlay Paw Wow Dancer bolo, artist unknown, no hallmark, 1950s-1960s, 1.72" x 2.97", $1000-1500.

VI.
Kachinas and Ceremonial Dancers from Other Tribes

As I noted earlier, there is a negative sanction against making any Kachina for sale in any medium, including silver jewelry. However, demand for the Kachina jewelry is huge, and Zuni artists have been forced to make it because they are deeply involved in the cash economy. They are requested to make it by traders. Moreover, they themselves might like to create this category of jewelry because this area may exactly and precisely satisfy their need for artistic expression. The best way to avoid violating the taboo is to make Kachinas from other tribes. Consequently, Hopi Snake Dancer, Hopi Butterfly Maiden, Apache Mountain Spirit Dancer, Pueblo Clown, and others have been made.

Hopi Butterfly Maiden

The Hopi Butterfly Maiden has been created by various Hopi Kachina carvers. In Zuni jewelry, Walter Nahktewa made a Hopi Butterfly Maiden pin in 1929 (Sotheby Park Bernet, 1975, pp. 80-81, #442). A similar Butterfly Maiden pin by an unknown Zuni artist was probably made in the 1970s-1980s (Bahti, 1992, p.29).

On page 124 is a Hopi Butterfly Maiden bolo probably made by Mary Kallestewa in the mosaic overlay style in the 1950s-1960s. I bought it at a gallery in Gallup. The gallery wrote on its back: "circa 1950's Leo Poblano." Just after I got it, I showed it to one of the oldest active artists, and he told me it was Mary Kallestewa's without hesitation. Although one informant attributed it to Dexter Cellicion, after close examination of this piece with my knowledgeable Zuni friend, we concluded it should be attributed to Mary Kallestewa, based on the raised mosaic inlay style. The face, forehead decoration and necklace are set slightly higher than the remaining parts, and the complex inlay work in her Tablita is unique. Whoever made it, it is one of the best examples of Zuni mosaic jewelry. It measures 4.56 inches tall and consists of blue turquoise, red coral, white mother-of-pearl, and black jet.

Mosaic overlay Hopi Butterfly Maiden bolo, Mary Kallestewa, no hallmark, 1950s-1960s, 5.18" x 4.56", $4000-6000.

Mary Kallestewa made this Hopi Butterfly Maiden bolo in the mosaic inlay style in the 1950s-1960s. It has smaller identical figures for its bolo tips, which one of my informants put on her ears as if they were earrings and enjoyed them greatly. However, she did not know who made this bolo. These figures seem to be made by the same artist who made the bolo just described: Mary Kallestewa. They are both made in the same manner, but the mosaic pattern in this Tablita is plainer than that of the former bolo. The bolo slide and bolo tips measure 4.59 and 1.79 inches, respectively. The slide consists of blue turquoise, red spiny oyster, white mother-of-pearl, gold lip mother-of-pearl, and black jet.

Mosaic overlay Hopi Butterfly Maiden bolo, Mary Kallestewa, no hallmark, 1950s-1960s, 4.78" x 4.59", $4000-6000.

This Hopi Butterfly Maiden bolo was made by Mary Kallestewa in the mosaic overlay style in the 1940s-1950s. It is made in almost identical pattern with the bolo just described. Because of its smaller size, there are five feathers over the Tablita. It measures 2.39 inches tall and consists of blue turquoise, orange spiny oyster, white mother-of-pearl, and black jet.

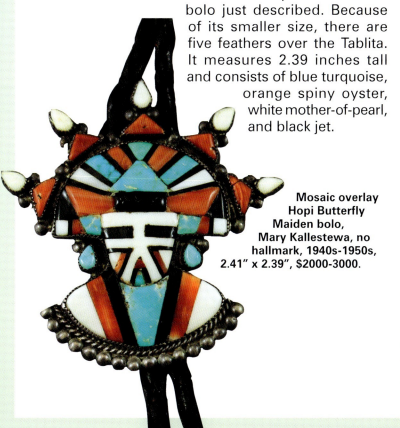

Mosaic overlay Hopi Butterfly Maiden bolo, Mary Kallestewa, no hallmark, 1940s-1950s, 2.41" x 2.39", $2000-3000.

Hopi Snake Dancer

The Snake Ceremony has been held at Hopi Pueblos. Webb and Weinstein (1973, p. 85) write:

> The snake ceremony is held on alternate years, with the intervening years taken up with the flute ceremony. On odd-numbered years the ceremony is held at Walpi on First Mesa and Mishongnovi on Second Mesa; on even-numbered years it was held in Oraibi, but in more recent times has been held in Hotevilla.

A. C. Vroman took many pictures of the ceremony in 1895, 1897, 1898, 1900, 1901, and 1902 and left field notes on the ceremony. According to his notes, the ceremony's main participants are the Chief Snake Priest and other priests of the Snake Order. As to their appearance, Vroman writes: "Their limbs and bodies are stained almost to a brown with some oxcide, chins painted white with black and white lightening stripes on bodies and limbs."

As to the dance itself, he says: "The snake carrier danced with his eyes shut apparently while he carried the snake in his mouth. When he would make the circuit of the plaza twice, he would drop his snake and pick up others that other dancers dropped, and so it would continue for about fifteen minutes."

The Snake Ceremony is held as an extremely sacred one by Snake priests, and is probably for water or rain. Because of the bad manner by the outsiders, the ceremony has been sometimes closed to the whites and any drunken Indians.

Hopi Snake Dancer in Zuni Jewelry

The C. G. Wallace Collection of American Indian Art auction catalog features three Snake Dancer figures: A bolo made by Leo Poblano on 1945 (#471), a bolo made by Jose Bowannie in 1938 (#194), and a pin made by Walter Nahktewa in 1929 (#838). As early as 1929, a Snake Dancer figure was made in the mosaic overlay or inlay style. Of these three figures, only the photo of Leo Poblano's Snake Dancer is featured.

This figure has a poisonous snake in both hands and his mouth and raises his right knee slightly in the air, while his left foot stands firmly on the ground. An animal fur hangs from his waist to his left side, and his body is painted black except for his white chin. There seems to be a white and red circle on his chest and zigzag pattern on his kilt. The kilt pattern symbolizes a snake. There are colorful feather ornaments on the head. This might be a prototype of Leo Poblano's Snake Dancer design.

There are other two Snake Dancer photos in *Jewelry by Southwest American Indians: Evolving Design* (Nancy N. Schiffer, 1990, p. 97). The Snake Dancer in the upper left corner is almost identical with Leo Poblano's Snake Dancer figure mentioned just above. The only differences are that Leo's Snake Dancer has an eagle feather in his left hand, and there is carving on the lower edge of the kilt. This is Leo Poblano's Snake Dancer made in the 1940s for sure. Another Snake Dancer figure in the lower right corner of the page is totally different from the two figures made by Poblano. Although its design is the same as Leo's first figure, it was clearly made by another excellent artist in the 1940s. The artist might be either Jose Bowannie or Walter Nahktewa. There is a white, snake-like design on the kilt. Moreover, the body construction is anatomically right and has a lot of muscles. He was an excellent artist.

There is another book (Rosenek and Stacy, 1976, the photo page between 86 and 87) which features two Snake Dancer figures along with many Kachinas and Ceremonial Dancers made by various artists. These two Snake Dancer figures are similar to the one made by Leo Poblano. Their postures, faces, hair decorations, arms, legs, moccasin covers, and animal furs are closely similar. However, the designs on their kilts are totally different. While Poblano's figure has a zigzag form which stands for a snake, these two figures do not have that form but a combination of many triangular parts in common. I believe they are made by Edward Beyuka, based on this kilt design.

I found another Snake Dancer bolo on a homepage of an online gallery. This bolo is attributed to Edward Beyuka, and the information says it is made in 1955. It is extremely similar to the one made by Leo Poblano, except for his kilt pattern. The dancer has a black face with turquoise inlaid eyes, carved nose, long hair, colorful hair decorations, muscular arms with turquoise bracelets and feathers, animal fur hanging from his waist, a kilt with carved sash, and red moccasins with carved white covers. His upper body is painted in black, and a red circular pattern is depicted with an encircling white band, which can also be seen on Leo Poblano's Snake Dancer figure.

This Snake Dancer bolo was made by one of the best representative lapidaries in the famous C. G. Wallace collection, Leo Poblano, in the mosaic inlay style in the 1940s-1950s, based on two circular and one W-shaped wire clasps. Compared with the Snake Dancer figure (#471) in the *The C. G. Wallace Collection of American Indian Art* auction catalog, they have basic features in common while they have minor differences as well. Their commonalities include a snake in both hands and his mouth, small white chins, five colorful hair ornaments, eagle feathers hanging from the back of their heads, furs hangings from their waist, turquoise necklaces and bracelets, lifted right legs, and white moccasin covers. The zigzag designs in their kilts and curved faces, hairs, necklace, bracelet, and moccasin covers are also in common. These common features demonstrate strongly that they are made by Leo Poblano. However, this dancer shows the circular painting on his upper body completely, no decoration in the lower end of his kilt, and black zigzag design sandwiched by two silver platelets, while the figure #471 shows half of his circular painting on his chest, zigzag design sandwiched by two white mother-of-pearl parts, and carved decoration in the lower end of his kilt. The figure measures 3.75 inches tall and consists of green turquoise, white mother-of-pearl, red spiny oyster, black jet, abalone shell, and pink shell.

Hopi Snake Dancer bolo, mosaic inlay, Leo Poblano, no hallmark, 1940s-1950s, 2" x 3.75", $4000-6000.

Leo Poblano made this Hopi Snake Dancer bolo in the mosaic inlay style in the 1940s-1950s, based on two round and one W-shaped wire clasps. The figure has one snake in his mouth, another one in his left hand, and one more snake in his right hand. He raises his right leg very slightly. There is a red zigzag design sandwiched by white mother-of-pearl parts in his kilt and carved turquoise decoration in the lower end of his kilt. He has full round painting on his chest as well. The figure measures 4.63 inches tall and consists of green turquoise, white mother-of-pearl, red spiny oyster, black jet, abalone shell, and orange shell.

Hopi Snake Dancer bolo, mosaic inlay, Leo Poblano, no hallmark, 1940s-1950s, 2.5" x 4.625", $5000-7500.

This Hopi Snake Dancer bolo was made by Leo Poblano in the mosaic inlay style in the late 1950s, just before his tragic death. The figure has a dangerous poisonous snake in his mouth, one eagle feather in his left hand, and a white fir branch in his right hand. This snake dancer figure has carvings on his hair, hair decorations, bracelets, moccasin covers, bottom edge of kilt, and face. Two turquoise eyes are inlaid, and his nose is carved higher from his facial surface. These are common features of Poblano's Snake Dancer figures. There is a zigzag design in his kilt as well. However, it is not sandwiched by two white mother-of-pearl parts and has only one part. Black jet is used only for hair and leg decorations in this figure, and tortoise shell is used for his face, hair, upper body, and kilt. It measures 3.875 inches tall and consists of green turquoise, red spiny oyster, white mother-of-pearl, black jet, abalone shell, and turtle shell.

The previous three Hopi Snake Dancer bolos have three-dimensionally curved faces, hairs, snakes, bracelets, necklaces, and feathers on their heads. After the completion of a formal training of sculpture by Daisy Hooee Nampeyo (Leo Poblano's first wife) at the Ecole de Beaus Art in

Hopi Snake Dancer bolo, mosaic inlay, Leo Poblano, no hallmark, late 1950s, 2.125"x 3.875", $3000-4500.

Paris, Nampeyo and Leo Poblano experimented on their lapidary works greatly. The zigzag designs in their kilts, symbolizing snakes, are the important point in which Hopi Snake Dancer figures made by Leo Poblano are distinguished from the ones by Edward Beyuka, although Edward Beyuka's earlier Snake Dancer figures are very similar. Even Madeline Beyuka, Edward's wife, misidentified my three Leo Poblano's figures as Edward's. Leo Poblano's step-daughter, Shirley Benn, attributed these three to Edward Beyuka as well, based on the curved white moccasin covers.

    I have seen four similar Snake Dancer pieces made by the same artist, two of which are bolos. One of them measures 3.125 inches tall, and the other one is 4.375 inches long. These pieces are sometimes misattributed to Leo Poblano by galleries or auction sellers. However, I have strong objection to this attribution, because these four Hopi Snake Dancer figures have common features that are clearly different from the features of Leo Poblano's. First, while Leo's pieces have muscular body constructions, these pieces have thin body constructions.

Hopi Snake Dancer bolo, mosaic inlay, John Lucio, no hallmark, 1950s-1960s, 1.25"x 2.75", $600-900.

Second, while Leo's pieces have lapidary snakes in their hands, these pieces have silver snakes. Third, while Leo's pieces have zigzag pattern in their kilts, these pieces have black curvilinear pattern in their kilts. Nevertheless, they all follow the same general Hopi Snake Dancer design. These Snake Dancers were attributed to John Lucio by my informants, and I agree with this attribution because his famous Eagle Dancers have this kind of thin body construction in common.

    This Snake Dancer bolo was made by John Lucio in the mosaic inlay style in the 1950s-1960s, based on the "Bennett Pat. Pend. C31" on the moving part of bolo clasp. This figure is almost identical with the pin on the next page, although this bolo is a little taller (2.75 inches) and the right arm of figure is not red-and black but all red. It consists of blue turquoise, red coral, white mother-of-pearl, iridescent abalone, and black jet.

    John Lucio made the Hopi Snake Dancer pin on page 130 in the mosaic inlay style in the late 1950s-1960s. Dancer's nose, hair, hair ornament and the bottom edge of the kilt are set a bit higher from the other parts of the figure. This pin measures 1.125 inches wide and 2.5 inches long and consists of blue turquoise, red coral, white mother-of-pearl, and black jet. The special feature of this pin is that the face is three-dimensionally curved; its nose sticks out from its surface, and two white eyes are inlaid. From the left side of his waist, an animal fur is hung. Considering its size, this Snake Dancer is impressive and attractive in its own right, even if it may not be as attractive as Leo's Snake Dancer figures.

Hopi Snake Dancer pin, mosaic inlay, John Lucio, no hallmark, 1950s-1960s, 1.125" x 2.5", $500-750.

This Hopi Snake Dancer bolo was made by John Lucio in the mosaic inlay style in the 1950s-1960s. Its lapidary work is almost identical with that of the pin described just above, while its silver work, especially that of snake, shows some clear differences. It measures 2.58 inches tall and consists of blue turquoise, red coral, white mother-of-pearl and black jet.

Hopi Snake Dancer bolo, mosaic inlay, John Lucio, no hallmark, 1950s-1960s, 1.20" x 2.58", $600-900.

As I discussed earlier, Snake Dancer pieces made by Edward Beyuka in the 1950s are very difficult to distinguish from those made by Leo Poblano in the 1940s-1950s. Even Shirley Benn and Madeline Beyuka misattributed my three Snake Dancer bolos to Edward Beyuka. Shirley Benn attributed them to Edward Beyuka because the white moccasin covers looked identical with Edward's.

This Snake Dancer bolo was made by Edward Beyuka in the mosaic inlay style in the 1970s-1980s. This piece can be more easily distinguished from the ones made by Leo Poblano. Stamped silver platelets in his waist and elbows and triangular parts in the lower half of his kilt are characteristic to Beyuka's Snake Dancer figures. Moreover, there is no zigzag pattern which signifies a snake clearly. It consists of blue turquoise, red coral, white mother-of-pearl, yellow clam shell, and black jet, and measures 4.5 inches tall.

Hopi Snake Dancer bolo, mosaic inlay, Edward Beyuka, EAB ZUNI, 1970s-1980s, 2.25" x 4.5", $1000-1500.

Apache Mountain Spirit Dancer

The Apache Mountain Spirit Dancer has been made by many Zuni mosaic inlay/overlay artists.

Mountain Spirit Dancers appear on the last day of the four-day maidens' puberty rite: the most important ceremony of the Apaches (Tom Bahti, 1968, pp. 48-53). They are accompanied by a crown who wears smaller version of the Mountain Spirit Dancer mask.

John Lucio made this Apache Mountain Spirit Dancer bolo in the mosaic inlay style in the 1940s-1950s. The black mask, black belt, black edge of the kilt and moccasins are set slightly higher than the remaining body, and three white dots representing eyes and mouth are inlaid. The stamped silver drops over the clown are unique to Lucio. It measures 2.75 inches tall and consists of green turquoise, red spiny oyster, white mother-of-pearl iridescent abalone, and black jet.

Apache Mountain Spirit Dancer bolo, mosaic inlay, John Lucio, no hallmark, 1940s-1950s, 2.125" x 2.75", $800-1200.

131

This Apache Mountain Spirit Dancer pin was made by John Lucio in the mosaic inlay style in the 1940s-1950s. This pin and the previous bolo are apparently made by the same artist. The mask, belt, the edge of the kilt, moccasins, and the blue part of the clown are set slightly higher than the body. Although there is no stamp on the silver drops over the clown, the four stamped silver drops around the Dancer's feet suggest that the piece is by Lucio. It measures 2.52 inches tall and consists of blue turquoise, red spiny oyster, white mother-of-pearl, iridescent abalone, and black jet.

Apache Mountain Spirit Dancer pin, mosaic inlay, John Lucio, no hallmark, 1940s-1950s, 1.87" x 2.52", $600-900.

This Apache Mountain Spirit Dancer bolo in the mosaic inlay style, probably from the 1940s-1950s, was made by an unknown artist. This originally was a pin and later converted to a bolo. His kilt and mask are set slightly higher than his body. His posture is similar to the previous two pieces made by John Lucio. One informant attributed it to him, but I am not sure about this attribution. It measures 3 inches tall and consists of blue turquoise, orange spiny oyster, white mother-of-pearl, iridescent abalone, and black jet.

Apache Mountain Spirit Dancer bolo converted from pin, mosaic inlay, artist unknown, no hallmark, 1940s-1950s, 2" x 3", $1000-1500.

Frank Vacit made this Apache Mountain Spirit Dancer ring in the mosaic inlay in mother-of-pearl style in the 1950s. It has his "ear of corn" hallmark on the back. It measures 0.92 inches wide and 1.81 inches tall. In this narrow space, a colorful dancing figure is intricately inlaid. This is my first Apache Mountain Spirit Dancer piece made by Frank Vacit, and I have seen this design of his for the first time. It consists of green turquoise, red coral, yellow olive shell, white mother-of-pearl, and black jet.

Apache Mountain Spirit Dancer ring, mosaic inlay, Frank Vacit, his "ear of corn" hallmark, 1950s, 0.92" x 1.81", $300-450.

This Apache Mountain Spirit Dancer pendant was made by Elliot Qualo in the mosaic inlay in mother-of-pearl style in the 1970s-1980s. The stamped silver edge and the bezel are unique to him, and there is a double antler hallmark on the back. His silver and lapidary work is beautifully done, with a lot of etching. Not surprisingly, he was selected as a member of Arizona Highways Magazine Hall of Fame. It measures 2.25 inches tall and consists of blue turquoise, red coral, white mother-of-pearl, and dark brown pen shell.

Apache Mountain Spirit Dancer pendant, mosaic inlay in mother-of-pearl, Elliot Qualo, double antler horns with ZUNI NM, 1970s-1980s, 1.75" x 2.25", $600-900.

Elliot Qualo made this Apache Mountain Spirit Dancer buckle in the mosaic inlay in tortoise shell style in the 1970s. There are a lot of incised lines all over the figure. Even his right hand is incised to show his individual fingers. His kilt is precisely incised as well. The stamps on the edge of the buckle and the form of bezel are unique to Qualo. The buckle back has his double antler hallmark but does not have any other mark. It measures 2.82 inches tall and consists of blue turquoise, red coral, white mother-of-pearl, gold lip mother-of-pearl, and black jet.

Apache Mountain Spirit Dancer buckle, mosaic inlay in tortoise shell, Elliot Qualo, double antler horns, 1970s-1980s, 3.55" x 2.82", $600-900.

This Apache Mountain Spirit Dancer ring was probably made by Elliott Qualo in the mosaic inlay in mother-of-pearl style in the 1950s-1960s. It measures only 1.09 inches tall. Considering this minute size, Qualo's lapidary work is incredible. The dancer extends both arms widely and stands still. It consists of green turquoise, red coral, white mother-of-pearl, and dark brown tortoise shell.

Apache Mountain Spirit Dancer ring, mosaic inlay in mother-of-pearl, Elliot Qualo, no hallmark, 1950s-1960s, 0.74" x 1.09", $100-150.

Anna Rita and Lambert Homer, Jr., made this Apache Mountain Spirit Dancer shell in the mosaic inlay in outer mother-of-pearl shell in the early 1960s. It won the first prize at the Inter-tribal Indian Ceremonial in 1963. There are two dancers: The larger one is inlaid on the highest part of the shell, and the much smaller one is set on his right side. This setting makes us feel the deepness of the scene. This is an extremely special version of their Mountain Spirit Dancer design. It measures 5.24 inches tall and consists of blue turquoise, red coral, white mother-of-pearl, a yellow shell, and black jet.

This Apache Mountain Spirit Dancer pin was made by Lambert Homer, Jr., and Anna Rita Homer in the mosaic inlay in tortoise shell style in the 1960s. There is an apparent resemblance between this figure and the larger figure on shell described just above. On July 6, 2011, Anna Rita Homer confirmed it was their work, made in the 1960s. A friend gave them a huge tortoise shell, and they made many pieces, including this pin, using the shell. The Dancer extends his legs and arms widely and stands still. We cannot feel his fierce movement. On this point, their figure is quite different from the one made by Elliott Qualo. In spite of this fact, their Apache Mountain Spirit Dancer pieces are beautifully designed and executed. It measures 2.46 inches tall and consists of blue turquoise, red coral, white mother-of-pearl, yellow olive shell, yellow and brown tortoise shell, and black jet.

Mosaic inlay in tortoise shell Apache Mountain Spirit Dancer pin, Lambert Homer Jr. and Anna Rita Homer, no hallmark, 1960s, 2.08" x 2.46", $400-600.

Mosaic inlay in mother of pearl shell Apache Mountain Spirit Dancer shell, mosaic inlay in outer mother of pearl shell, Lambert Homer Jr. and Anna Rita Homer, no hallmark, 1960s, 5.76" x 5.24", $2000-3000.

The lapidary work on this Apache Mountain Spirit Dancer bolo was by Lambert Homer, Jr., and Anna Rita Homer in the 1980s, and the silver work was by Curtis Kucate in 2011. When, in July 2011, I asked Anna Rita Homer to confirm whether the Apache Mountain Spirit Dancer pin described just above was made by them, she showed me this insert. As Dancer's eyes were not etched, I asked her to complete it and sell the piece to me. It measures 1.94 inches tall and consists of blue turquoise, red coral, white mother-of-pearl, and black jet.

Mosaic inlay in mother-of-pearl shell Apache Mountain Spirit Dancer bolo, Lambert Homer Jr. and Anna Rita Homer for the inserts and Curtis Kucate for silver work, no hallmark, 1980s and 2011 respectively, 1.53" x 1.94", $300-450.

This is an Apache Mountain Spirit Dancer pendant with inlay work by Anna Rita and Lambert Homer, Jr., in the mosaic inlay in mother-of-pearl in the mid-1980s and the silver work by Curtis Kucate in 2011. When I visited Anna Rita Homer to interview her in September 2010, she sold me this insert, which she inlaid just before her husband passed on. I asked my friend, Curtis Kucate, to make it into a pendant. This is the standard design of their Apache Mountain Spirit Dancer, allowing us to identify their pieces. As they are not silversmiths but lapidaries, their works have been mounted on silver by various Zuni and Navajo silversmiths. It measures 1.29 inches tall excluding the bale and consists of blue turquoise, red coral, white mother-of-pearl, and black jet.

Mosaic inlay in mother-of-pearl shell Apache Mountain Spirit Dancer pendant, Lambert Homer, Jr., and Anna Rita Homer for insert and Curtis Kucate for silver work, no hallmark, 1980s and 2011, respectively, 0.96" x 1.29", $120-180.

On this Apache Mountain Spirit Dancer ring with the inlay work was by Anna Rita and Lambert Homer, Jr., in the mosaic inlay in mother-of-pearl shell style in the 1970s-1980s. It was confirmed as theirs by Anna Rita Homer in July 2011. The silver work and turquoise and coral cabochon setting might be done by a Navajo silversmith with the initial "IB." The insert is 0.69 inches wide and 1.28 inches tall. The total ring measures 2.36 inches tall, and blue turquoise and pink coral cabochons are set around the insert. The insert consists of blue turquoise, red coral, white mother-of-pearl, and black jet.

Leonard and Edith Lonjose made this Apache Mountain Spirit Dancer bolo in the mosaic inlay in mother-of-pearl style in the 1950s-1960s. An almost identical piece appears in *Zuni: the Art and the People* (Bell, 1975, p. 31). The dancer's kilt is set slightly higher than the remaining part. His head is round, while a similar Apache Mountain Spirit Dancer made by Tony Ohmsatte has a flat head. The silver work done by Leonard is much more decorative than any other Zuni silversmiths. It measures 2.05 inches tall and consists of blue/green turquoise, red spiny oyster, white mother-of-pearl, and black jet.

Mosaic inlay in mother-of-pearl shell Apache Mountain Spirit Dancer ring, Lambert Homer Jr. and Anna Rita Homer and a Navajo silver smith, IB, 1970s-1980s, 1.26" x 2.36", $120-180.

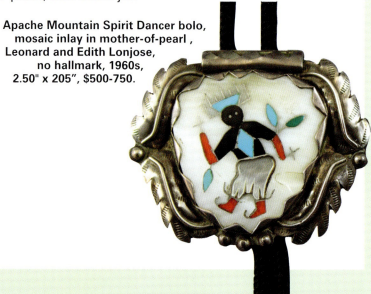

Apache Mountain Spirit Dancer bolo, mosaic inlay in mother-of-pearl , Leonard and Edith Lonjose, no hallmark, 1960s, 2.50" x 205", $500-750.

This Apache Mountain Spirit Dancer bolo was made by Leonard and Edith Lonjose in the mosaic inlay in mother-of-pearl style in the 1950s-1960s. Two dancers are dancing while bending their bodies in opposite directions. The contrast of different sizes of the Dancers gives this bolo perspective. It measures 2.43 inches tall and consists of blue turquoise, red spiny oyster, white mother-of-pearl, and black jet.

Leonard and Edith Lonjose made this Apache Mountain Spirit Dancer bracelet in the mosaic inlay in mother-of-pearl style in the 1970s. Each Apache Mountain Spirit Dancer is inlaid in a rectangular mother-of-pearl shell. The dancers are set in the channels dug in the silver cuff bracelet. This construction reminds me of the one made by Tony Ohmsatte, but the work of the Lonjoses seems older. The rectangular insert measures 1.34 inches tall and consists of blue turquoise, red spiny oyster, yellow fossilized walrus ivory, and black jet.

Apache Mountain Spirit Dancer bolo, mosaic inlay in mother-of-pearl , Leonard and Edith Lonjose, no hallmark, 1950s-1960s, 2.47" x 2.43", $800-1200.

Apache Mountain Spirit Dancer bracelet, mosaic inlay in mother-of-pearl , Lonard and Edith Lonjose, Lonjose L + E ZUNI and Cloud and Rain symbol, 1970s-1980s, 1.125" x 1.375" for the inserts, $600-900.

137

This Apache Mountain Spirit Dancer ring was made by Leonard and Edith Lonjose in the mosaic inlay in mother-of-pearl style in the 1960s-1970s. The ring face measures 1.15 inches tall and consists of blue turquoise, red spiny oyster, yellow fossilized walrus ivory, and black jet.

Apache Mountain Spirit Dancer ring, mosaic inlay in mother-of-pearl , Lonard and Edith Lonjose, no hallmark, 1960s-190s, 0.88" x 1.15", $100-150.

Tony Ohmsatte made this Apache Mountain Spirit Dancer bracelet in the mosaic inlay in mother-of-pearl style in the 1970s-1980s. His design is similar with the one made by Leonard and Edith Lonjose. However, as I described earlier, his Mountain Spirit Dancer has a head that is flat on top, while the work of the Lonjoses use a round head. In addition, the forms of lines which start from the crown are different. The rectangular inlaid insert measures 1.15 inches tall, and consists of blue turquoise, red coral, yellow melon shell, dark brown pen shell, and black jet.

Apache Mountain Spirit Dancer bracelet, mosaic inlay in mother-of-pearl , Tony Ohmsatte, Tony Ohmsatte, 1970s-1980s, 1" x 1.125" for the inserts, $400-600.

A matching Apache Mountain Spirit Dancer ring was made by Tony Ohmsatte in the mosaic inlay in mother-of-pearl style in the 1970s-1980s. It measures 1.16 inches tall and consists of blue turquoise, red coral, yellow melon shell, dark brown pen shell, and black jet.

Apache Mountain Spirit Dancer ring, mosaic inlay in mother-of-pearl , Tony Ohmsatte, T Ohmsatte, 1970s-1980s, 1" x 1.125" for the inserts, $150-225.

This Apache Mountain Spirit Dancer bracelet was made by Tony Ohmsatte in the mosaic inlay in mother-of-pearl style in the 1970s-1980s. It is signed "T. O. Zuni" with electric pen. The insert measures 1.23 inches tall and consists of blue turquoise, red coral, yellow melon shell, and black jet. Tony Ohmsatte does not use pen shell in this piece.

Apache Mountain Spirit Dancer bracelet, mosaic inlay in MOP, Tony Ohmsatte, T. O. Zuni, 1970s-1980s, 1.02" x 1.23" for the inserts, $400-600.

Vera Luna made this Apache Mountain Spirit Dancer bolo in the mosaic inlay style in the 1970s-1980s. The mask and belt are set slightly higher than the rest of the figure, and two turquoise dots and one coral dot are inlaid for eyes and mouth in the mask. The dancer raises his right knee and right arm slightly and puts down his left arm. It measures 4.08 inches tall and consists of blue turquoise, red coral, white mother-of-pearl, yellow melon shell, iridescent abalone, and black jet.

Apache Mountain Spirit Dancer bolo, mosaic inlay in mother-of-pearl , Vera Luna, V. Luna, 1970s-1980s, 2.26" x 4.08", $400-600.

This Apache Mountain Spirit Dancer stick pin was made by Vera Luna in the mosaic inlay style in the 1970s-1980s. The figure, excluding pin, measures 1.23 inches tall and consists of blue turquoise, red coral, gold lip mother-of-pearl, and black jet.

Apache Mountain Spirit Dancer stick pin, mosaic inlay in mother-of-pearl, Vera Luna, V. L., 1970s-1980s, 0.77" x 1.23", $100-150.

Virgil and Shirley Benn made this Apache Mountain Spirit Dancer bolo in the mosaic inlay style in 2010. The dancer puts both hands down and raises his left knee very slightly. With these limited physical features, the posture still shows a feeling of movement. The bird symbol on his crown enhances the attractiveness of this figure. It measures 4.81 inches tall and consists of blue turquoise, red spiny oyster, white mother-of-pearl, yellow melon shell, and black jet.

Mosaic inlay Apache Mountain Spirit Dancer bolo, Virgil and Shirley Benn, V. & S. Benn, 2010, 2.60" x 4.81", $1200-1800.

Other Hopi Kachinas

Zuni people have Sun Kachina, but I have seen few Sun Kachina in jewelry so far. I own two Sun Kachinas, but they are all Hopi Sun Kachinas according to my Zuni friends.

This Hopi Sun Kachina bolo was made by Andrew Dewa in the mosaic overlay style in the 1980s-1990s. His style is the raised mosaic overlay, and we cannot see any silver from the front. We can see silver bezels only when we view the figure from its side. This may be an extremely difficult technique to execute. The Kachina has a gourd in his right hand and a flower-like object in his left hand and stands still. This bolo measures 3.08 inches tall and consists of blue turquoise, red coral, white mother-of-pearl, gold lip mother-of-pearl, iridescent abalone, and black jet.

Mosaic overlay Hopi Sun Kachina bolo, Andrew Dewa, A DEWA ZUNI, 1980s-1990s, 1.26" x 3.08", $800-1200.

Adrian Bowannie made this Hopi Sun Kachina pin in the mosaic inlay style in the 1950s-1960s. He has a gourd in his left hand and stands still. It measures 2.82 inches tall and consists of blue/green turquoise, red spiny oyster, white mother-of-pearl, gold lip mother-of-pearl, and black jet.

Mosaic overlay Hopi Sun Kachina pin, Adrian Bowannie, no hallmark, 1950s-1960s, 2.11" x 2.82", $300-400.

This Hopi Rain Bird Kachina bolo was made by Frank Vacit in the silver overlay/mosaic inlay style in the 1980s-1990s. The Kachina's face, collar, and lower arms are all blue, and a red beak is evident. In addition, we can feel his forward movement in this bolo. Two diagonal belts run from each shoulder across to the waist. This is an extremely well-made piece. It measures 2.17 inches tall and consists of blue turquoise, red coral, white mother-of-pearl, and black jet.

Silver overlay/mosaic inlay Hopi Rain Bird Kachina bolo, Frank Vacit, F VACIT-ZUNI and his "ear of corn" hallmark, 1980s-1990s, 1.90" x 2.17", $1000-1500.

Frank Vacit made this Hopi Morning Kachina bolo in the silver overlay/mosaic inlay style in the 1950s-1960s. It is an elaborately made bolo, depicting the bust of the Kachina. The Kachina has a big red ears and black-and-white feathers which resemble the Wotemthla Kachina. However, he wears a white ceremonial gown and tri-colored accessories (blue-black-red). This costume rather seems to remind us more of Hopi Morning Kachina. The silver stamps on both sides are Vacit's, owned by one of his daughters now. It measures 2.03 inches tall and consists of green turquoise, red spiny oyster, white mother-of-pearl, black jet, and a yellow shell.

Silver overlay/mosaic inlay Hopi Morning Kachina bolo, Frank Vacit, his "ear of corn" hallmark, 1940s-1950s, 1.49" x 1.46", $800-1200.

This Hopi Morning Kachina bolo was made by Andrew Dewa in the mosaic overlay style in the 1980s-1990s. Kachina has a megaphone-like object in his right hand and a flower-like object (also regularly held by his Sun Kachina) in his left hand and stands still. We cannot feel any movement in his posture. It measures 5.38 inches tall and consists of blue turquoise, red coral, white mother-of-pearl, gold lip mother-of-pearl, dark green serpentine, and black jet.

Mosaic overlay Hopi Morning Kachina bolo, Andrew Dewa, A DEWA ZUNI, 1980s-1990s, 1.91" x 5.38", $1500-2250.

Joe Zunie made this Hopi Basket Dancer bolo in the mosaic inlay style in the 1960s-1980s. Her necklace and white fir branch in the right hand are set higher than the rest of figure. By raising her right knee and right hand slightly, the dancer seems to gain liveliness. There are a lot of etchings all around this figure, which make this figure realistic. The bolo has identical baskets for bolo tips. It measures 5.68 inches tall and consists of green turquoise, red spiny oyster, white mother-of-pearl, gold lip mother-of-pearl, and black jet.

Mosaic inlay Hopi Basket Dancer bolo/pendant, Joe Zunie, JZJ Joe Zunie, 1960s-1980s, 2.52" x 5.68", $1500-2250.

This Hopi Hano Clown ring was made by Augustine and Rosalie Pinto in mosaic inlay in pen shell style in the 1970s-1980s. The total figure is inlaid slightly higher than the background. It measures 1.43 inches tall and consists of green turquoise, red coral, white mother-of-pearl, gold lip mother-of-pearl, and black jet.

Mosaic overlay Hano Clown ring, Augustine and Rosalie Pinto, ARP NM ZUNI, 1970s-1980s, 1.14" x 1.43", $120-180.

143

Beverley Etsate made this Hopi Hano Clown ring in the raised mosaic inlay in pen shell style in the 1990s-2000s. Her clown looks short and fat, compared with the one made by her parents, Augustine and Rosalie Pinto. It measures 1.33 inches tall and consists of blue turquoise, red coral, white mother-of-pearl, gold lip mother-of-pearl, and black jet.

Mosaic overlay Hano Clown pin/pendant, Beverly Etsate, Bev. Etsate ZUNI NM, 1990s-2000s, 1.12" x 1.33", $80-120.

Ceremonial Dancer from Mexico

This Aztec Dancer bolo was made by Joe Zunie in the mosaic inlay style in the 1960s. His necklace, gourd, moccasin cover and shield are set higher than the rest of the figure. There are a lot of etchings all around the figure, making this figure look natural. His posture and anatomical construction seem to give this figure feeling of strength and dynamics. The red and green cape enhances the attractiveness of this figure. It measures 4.53 inches tall and consists of green turquoise, red spiny oyster, white mother-of-pearl, gold lip mother-of-pearl, and black jet.

Mosaic inlay Aztec Dancer bolo, Joe Zunie, no hallmark, 1960s, 2.59" x 4.53", $1200-1800.

Joe Zunie also made this Aztec Dancer bolo in the mosaic inlay style in the 1970s-1980s. His necklace, bracelet, moccasin cover, and an ornament on the side of his face are set higher than the rest of the figure, and a lot of etchings are added all around the figure. His posture and anatomical construction make this figure look very strong and brave. It measures 5.83 inches tall and consists of blue turquoise, orange spiny oyster, white mother-of-pearl, gold lip mother-of-pearl, dark brown pen shell, and black jet.

Mosaic inlay Aztec Dancer bolo/pendant, Joe Zunie, JZJ Joe Zunie, 1970s-1980s, 3.39" x 5.83", $1500-2250.

VII.
Present Kachina Jewelry Artists

I would like to introduce three contemporary Kachina Jewelry artists who have been actively creating their own pieces in the mosaic inlay or overlay style.

Philander Gia

Philander Gia attended the Institute of American Indian Arts and had worked various jobs such as a furniture maker, carpenter, and seasonal firefighter. After retirement from firefighting, he did lapidary and silver work as a part-timer while working in carpentry. Now, he works full-time for this jewelry business. He has had a lot of backorders for his Kachina jewelry in the form of a bow guard from local residents in Zuni for religious dance. Consequently, I have had hard time getting my first one. When I saw a bow guard of Hopi Corn Kachina owned by my close friend, Keffe Chapella, I ordered the same one. It took more than a year to get it. Gia's pieces are conceived and executed very well. He will be a successor of the great Kachina jewelry artists such as Teddy Weahkee, Leo Poblano, John Lucio, Virgil and Shirley Benn, and Andrew Dewa.

This White Warrior Kachina bow guard was made by Philander Gia in the mosaic overlay style in the 2000s. It originally was a present to his son-in-law for a religious dance. When he asked Philander to make another bow guard, Philander sold it to me. It is my first bow guard made by him. I admire his creativity in design and execution. It measures 5.01 inches tall and consists of blue turquoise, red coral, white mother-of-pearl, white clam shell, green malachite, and an unknown brown stone.

Mosaic overlay White Warrior Kachina bow guard, Philander Gia, no hallmark, 2000s, 3.24" x 5.01", $700-1050.

Philander Gia made this Hopi Corn Kachina bow guard in the mosaic overlay style in 2011. I ordered this one a few years ago. As he had a full-time job in carpentry, he could not finish it for a long time. Finally, I got it in January 2011, along with the next bow guard. There are tadpoles depicted on his head and gourd and silver snakes all around the edge of the silver backing. This is an extremely well-conceived and well-executed piece in the cubic mosaic overlay technique. The details are etched and drawn on stone/shell parts. It measures 4.92 inches tall and consists of blue turquoise, red coral, pink coral, white mother-of-pearl, green malachite, dark brown pen shell, and an unknown brown stone.

Mosaic overlay Hopi Corn Kachina bow guard, Philander Gia, no hallmark, 2011, 3.15" x 4.92", $700-1050.

This Wotemthla Kachina bow guard was made by Philander Gia in the mosaic overlay style in January 2011. Details are etched and painted on stone/shell parts, which are set in the cubic way. It measures 5 inches tall and consists of green turquoise, red coral, spotted brown cowrie shell, dark brown pen shell, white mother-of-pearl, orange shell, and brown stone.

Mosaic overlay Wotemthla Kachina bow guard, Philander Gia, no hallmark, 2011, 3.18" x 5.00", $700-1050.

Philander Gia made this Hilili Kachina bow guard in the mosaic overlay style in April 2011. The Hilili Dance is performed in early spring. Fortunately, I was there to observe the dance in April 2011, at the Dance Plaza in Zuni Pueblo. Philander Gia told me he would make me a Hilili bow guard. I acquired it on the last day of my six day stay in Zuni. There is a butterfly etching on the round ornament on the right side of mask and four feathers on Kachina's left side. There are two long brown objects hanging down along both sides of the mask which seem to be snakes. It measures 3.19 inches tall and consists of blue turquoise, white mother-of-pearl, gold lip mother-of-pearl, dark brown pen shell, spotted brown cowrie shell, and red stone.

Mosaic overlay Hilili Kachina bow guard, Philander Gia, no hallmark, 2011, 4.50" x 3.19", $700-1050.

This Hututu bow guard was made by Philander Gia in the mosaic overlay style on July 11, 2011. I ordered a bow guard in this design in April 2011. The Kachina sets his left foot firmly on the red ground and raises his right knee high. He has feathers in his left hand and deer scapulae in his right hand (Bunzel, 1984, p. 962). He wears turquoise and red coral joclas from his neck and a bow guard with a turquoise nugget on his left wrist. It measures 4.81 inches tall and consists of blue turquoise, red coral, white mother-of-pearl, gold lip mother-of-pearl, green malachite, and black jet.

Mosaic overlay Hututu Kachina bow guard, Philander Gia, no hallmark, 2011, 3.16" x 4.81", $800-1200.

Philander Gia made this Yamuhakto bow guard in the mosaic overlay style on November 3, 2011. The Kachina stands still, holding deer antlers in his hands. He measures 4.37 inches tall and wears a bow guard and jocla necklace and wears a pair of colorful moccasins. The bow guard measures 5.04 inches tall and consists of blue turquoise, red coral, white mother-of-pearl, dark brown pen shell, brown pipe stone, and other shells.

Mosaic overlay Yamuhakto Kachina bow guard, Philander Gia, no hallmark, 2011, 3.14" x 5.36", $800-1200.

This is a Butterfly Maiden Dancer pin made by Philander Gia in the usual mosaic inlay style in April 2011. It is a smaller and cute piece. As her face is blue, she might be wearing a mask. It measures 2.74 inches tall and consists of blue turquoise, red coral, white mother-of-pearl, green malachite, and black jet.

Mosaic inlay Butterfly Maiden Kachina pin, Philander Gia, Philander Gia Zuni NM, 2011, 1.01" x 2.74", $160-240.

This White Feather Downy Kachina pin was made by Philander Gia in the mosaic overlay style on July 4, 2011. As described previously, this Kachina appears in the Rain Dance and is an alternate of Kokokshi Kachina along with Red Beard Kachina. I observed the Summer Mixed Dance on July 2, 2011, in which many Kokokshi and White Feather Downy Kachinas danced with some Gleasy boys, Apache Kachinas, and Mud Head Kachinas. This figure has an untied long hair like the Kokokshi Kachina and a long beard. On the beard, two big white feathers hang. The pendant measures 2.04 inches tall and consists of blue turquoise, red coral, white mother-of-pearl, gold lip mother-of-pearl, dark brown pen shell, and black jet.

Mosaic overlay White-Feather-Downy Kachina pendant, Philander Gia, Philander Gia Zuni NM, 2011, 1.52" x 2.04", $160-240.

Philander Gia made this Red Beard Kachina pendant in the mosaic overlay style on July 4, 2011. This figure is almost identical with the White-Feather-Downy Kachina except for his red beard and two brown feathers. It measures 2.06 inches tall and consists of blue turquoise, red spiny oyster, dark brown pen shell, yellow olive shell, white mother-of-pearl, gold lip mother-of-pearl, and black jet.

Mosaic overlay Red Beard Kachina pendant, Philander Gia, Philander Gia Zuni NM, 2011, 1.53" x 2.06", $160-240.

Andrea Lonjose Shirley

Andrea Lonjose Shirley learned how to make Kachina jewelry from the parents of her ex-husband, Virgil and Shirley Benn. She has been an accomplished Kachina jeweler for approximately 20 years.

Her Shulawitsi pin was made in the mosaic inlay style in 2010. He wears a female deer fur from his right shoulder across to his left waist, a bow guard around his left wrist, and a bracelet around his right wrist. A lot of colorful dots are inlaid all around his black body. Her inlay work is incredible. It measures 3.36 inches tall and consists of blue turquoise, red coral, white mother-of-pearl, gold lip mother-of-pearl, and black jet.

Andrea Lonjose Shirley made this Downy-Feather-Hanging Kachina pin in the mosaic inlay style in 2010. A fur hangs down from the back of his waist, and white feathers adorn his long hair and beard. His name originated from the white feathers on his beard. He has a gourd in his right hand and a white fir branch in his left hand. He stands still. Andrea executed this figure extremely beautifully. It measures 3.43 inches tall and consists of blue turquoise, red coral, w h i t e mother-of-pearl, gold lip mother-of-pearl, deep green malachite, and black jet.

Mosaic inlay Shulawitsi pin, Andrea Lonjose Shirley, ALS, 2010, 1.94" x 3.36", $300-450.

Mosaic inlay Downy Feathers Hanging Kachina pin, Andrea Lonjose Shirley, ALS Zuni Male Rain Dancer, 2010, 1.63" x 3.43", $300-450.

This Santo Domingo Kokokshi Girl pin was made by Andrea Lonjose Shirley in the mosaic inlay style in 2010. Andrea wrote "Female Rain Dancer" on the back, so this Kachina is a companion for the Downy Feather Hanging Kachina. The dancer has white fir branches in both hands and wears a white robe from her shoulder. It measures 3.52 inches tall and consists of blue turquoise, red coral, white mother-of-pearl, gold lip mother-of-pearl, deep green malachite, and black jet.

Mosaic inlay Kachina Girl pin, Andrea Lonjose Shirley, ALS Zuni Female Rain Dancer, 2010, 1.56" x 3.52", $300-450.

Andrea Lonjose Shirley made this Ram Kachina pin in the mosaic inlay style in 2010. Andrea wrote "Mountain Sheep Kachina" on the back. He has a gourd in his right hand and a white fir branch in his left and stands still. It measures 3.41 inches tall and consists of blue turquoise, red coral, white mother-of-pearl, gold lip mother-of-pearl, iridescent abalone, deep green malachite, and black jet.

Mosaic inlay Ram Kachina pin, Andrea Lonjose Shirley, ALS Zuni Mountain Sheep Kachina, 2010, 1.33" x 3.41", $300-450.

This is a Sky Kachina pin made by Andrea Lonjose Shirley in the mosaic inlay style in 2010. He has an animal-like snout and wears fur around his shoulder (Wright, 1985, pp. 94-95). He holds a gourd in his right hand and a yucca bundle in his left hand. There are fan-shaped eagle feathers and upright macaw plumes on the back of the head. He also raises his right knee slightly. It measures 3.45 inches tall and consists of blue turquoise, red coral, white mother-of-pearl, gold lip mother-of-pearl, iridescent abalone, deep green malachite, and black jet.

Mosaic inlay Sky Kachina pin, Andrea Lonjose Shirley, ALS Zuni Sky Kachina, 2010, 1.40" x 3.45", $300-450.

Andrea Lonjose Shirley made this Tomtsinapa pin in the mosaic inlay style in 2010. Tomtsinapa appears in the Laguna Chakwaina Dance and is famous for his sweet voice (Wright, 1985, pp. 103-104). He comes for the benefit of the women as well as good crops. He has a small spruce tree in his left hand (Wright, 1985, p. 104) and a gourd in his right hand

and raises his right knee slightly. On the top of the spruce tree, several feathers are attached. It measures 3.39 inches tall and consists of blue turquoise, red coral, white mother-of-pearl, gold lip mother-of-pearl, deep green malachite, and black jet.

Mosaic inlay Zuni Tomtsinapa Kachina pin, Andrea Lonjose Shirley, ALS Zuni Tomtsinapa Kachina, 2010, 1.44" x 3.39", $300-450.

This Ball Eye Kachina pin was made by Andrea Lonjose Shirley in the mosaic inlay style in 2010. He wears a warrior's bandoleer and carries a red gourd in his right hand (Wright, 1985, pp. 103-104). He has a long black beard and a long red hanging tongue. He raises his right knee slightly. It measures 3.39 inches tall and consists of blue turquoise, red coral, white mother-of-pearl, gold lip mother-of-pearl, deep green malachite, and black jet.

Mosaic inlay Zuni Eye Ball Kachina pin, Andrea Lonjose Shirley, ALS Zuni Eye Ball Kachina, 2010, 1.36" x 3.39", $300-450.

Andrea Lonjose Shirley made this Double-Faced Kachina pin in the mosaic inlay style in 2010. He is one of the little dancers that a younger boy impersonates. He has switches in both hands (Wright, 1985, pp. 108-109). It measures 3.39 inches tall and consists of blue turquoise, red coral, white mother-of-pearl, gold lip mother-of-pearl, iridescent abalone, deep green malachite, and black jet.

Mosaic inlay Zuni Double Faced Kachina pin, Andrea Lonjose Shirley, ALS Zuni Double-Faced Kachina, 2010, 1.36" x 3.39", $300-450.

This Ya'ana Kachina pin was made by Andrea Lonjose Shirley in the mosaic inlay style in 2010. His face is all black, and he has an ear of corn in each hand. When he appears, Koyemshi make fun of him (Wright, 1985, pp. 95-96). It measures 3.39 inches tall and consists of blue turquoise, red coral, white mother-of-pearl, gold lip mother-of-pearl, deep green malachite, and black jet.

Mosaic inlay Zuni Ya'ana Kachina pin, Andrea Lonjose Shirley, ALS Zuni Ya'ana Kachina, 2010, 1.52" x 3.39", $300-450.

Andrea Lonjose Shirley made this Corn Grinding Girl pin in the mosaic inlay style in 2010. This ceremony occurs at long erratic intervals on the last day of the summer dances (Wright, 1985, pp. 74-77). The girl has an ear of corn in each hand and is raising her right hand slightly. She is in the traditional female formal dress. It measures 3.39 inches tall and consists of blue turquoise, red coral, white mother-of-pearl, gold lip mother-of-pearl, iridescent abalone, deep green malachite, and black jet.

Mosaic inlay Zuni Corn Grinding Maiden Kachina pin, Andrea Lonjose Shirley, ALS Zuni Corn Grinding Maiden Kachina, 2010, 1.52" x 3.39", $300-450.

Eldred Martinez

Eldred Martinez used to make Kachina Jewelry with a lot of etchings. Recently, he has made a set of the Saiyatasha Party in the forms of pins and a necklace. The necklace I saw on an online catalog consisted of Shulawitsi for the center piece, Saiyatasha and Hututu next to it, and two Yamhakto on both ends.

His Saiyatasha pin was made in the mosaic inlay style in the 2010. This design reminds me of Red Leekela's pieces introduced in this book. His relatively shorter horn, rectangular turquoise decoration in the forehead, and red ornament on his right shoulder are similar to those of the pieces probably made by Red Leekela. The Kachina's face, collar and headband are set slightly higher than the rest, and etching is added on some of the black parts. It measures 2.52 inches tall and consists of blue turquoise, red spiny oyster, white mother-of-pearl, and black jet.

Mosaic inlay Saiyatasha pin/pendant, Eldred Martinez, Eldred Martinez ZUNI N. M., Zuni Long Horn, 2010, 2.16" x 2.52", $240-360.

Eldred Martinez made this Hututu pin in the mosaic inlay style in 2010. This design also reminds me of the one that I attributed to Red Leekela in this book, even though Red's piece is much smaller and has round ears. It measures 2.52 inches tall and consists of blue turquoise, red spiny oyster, white mother-of-pearl, and black jet.

Mosaic inlay Hututu pin/pendant, Eldred Martinez, Eldred Martinez ZUNI N. M., Wilo Do Do, 2010, 2.16" x 2.52", $240-360.

This Yamhakto pin was made by Eldred Martinez in the mosaic inlay style in 2010. He writes 'Zuni Wood Carrier' on its back. Yamhakto is a helper for Saiyatasha and Hututu, therefore, two Yamhaktos are strung in Martinez's necklace. It measures 2.54 inches tall and consists of blue turquoise, red spiny oyster, white mother-of-pearl, gold lip mother-of-pearl, and black jet.

Mosaic inlay Yamhakto pin/pendant, Eldred Martinez, Eldred Martinez ZUNI N. M., Zuni Wood Carrier, 2010, 1.81" x 2.54", $240-360.

This is a Shulawitsi pin made by Eldred Martinez in the mosaic inlay style in 2010. He wrote "Zuni Fire God" on the back. Shulawitsi is a little dancer that a little boy impersonates. Colorful dots are inlaid all over the mask. It measures 2.44 inches tall and consists of blue turquoise, red spiny oyster, white mother-of-pearl, gold lip mother-of-pearl, and black jet.

Mosaic inlay Shlawitsi pin/pendant, Eldred Martinez, Eldred Martinez ZUNI N. M., Zuni Fire God, 2010, 1.71" x 2.44", $240-360.

Conclusion

I have compiled and examined more than 240 Kachina jewelry pieces made by various Zuni artists. Some artists are very famous, while others are not. Compared with the designs such as Knifewing, Rainbow Man, Sun Face, and Hopi Bird, far fewer artists dare to create the Kachina jewelry, probably because there is a strong negative sanction against making the Kachina jewelry in precise and authentic manner for sale. Some artists remained anonymous because of this taboo while others dared to create it. Other artists tried to avoid violating the taboo by modifying an important part of a figure, and still others made Kachinas and Ceremonial Dancers from other pueblos and tribes.

Some Kachinas or Ceremonial Dancers, such as the Saiyatasha, Antelope Kachina, Eagle Dancers and Apache Gahn Dancer, are made by some artists while others such as Hopi Snake Dancer, Hututu and Salimopia are less commonly made.

The variation of the designs made by various artists is evident. There are clear variations in Kachina jewelry, as has been seen in Knifewing, Rainbow Man, Hopi Bird, and Sun Face pieces. An artist tries to be unique to become a true artist. He/She does not want to copy someone's design. Zuni cultural value for not copying someone else's design enforces this individual effort via gossip network. This is one of the main reasons that the variation is generated. At the same time, an outstanding individual artist such as Leo Poblano also owns the variation within their works. His Hopi Snake Dancer pieces seem to demonstrate this point well.

We have appreciated Kachina and Ceremonial Dancer figures made by several great artists, including Leo Poblano, Walter Nahktewa, Frank Vacit, Mary Kallestewa, John Lucio, Dexter Cellicion, Edward Beyuka, and Andrew Dewa. If we examine many more items made by Walter Nahktewa, he will be re-evaluated much more highly.

John Lucio should be evaluated much more highly as well. He has been best known only for his Eagle Dancers, but he made various marvelous Dancer figures in the 1940s-1950s, such as Apache Mountain Spirit Dancer, Hopi Snake Dancer and Hoop Dancer.

I hope more Zuni artists will choose to make Kachinas and Ceremonial Dancers in jewelry. As Kachinas and Ceremonial Dancers are important and sacred for Zuni people, they are some of the best gateways for the appreciation of the Zuni culture and an understanding of the Zuni people. They are fascinating, without a doubt.

References

Adair, John. *The Navajo and Pueblo Silversmiths*. Norman, Oklahoma: University of Oklahoma Press. 1944.

Arizona Highways. January 1945. Phoenix, Arizona: The Arizona Highway Department. 1945.

Arizona Highways. August 1952. Phoenix, Arizona: The Arizona Department of Transportation. 1952.

Arizona Highways. August 1959. Phoenix, Arizona: The Arizona Department of Transportation. 1959.

Arizona Highways. August 1974. Phoenix, Arizona: Arizona Department of Transportation. 1974.

Bahti, Tom. *Southwestern Indian Tribes*. Las Vegas, Nevada: KC Publications. 1968.

Bassman, Theda and Michael. *Zuni Jewelry*. Atglen, Pennsylvania: Schiffer Publishing, Ltd. 1999.

Baxter, Paula A. *Southwest Silver Jewelry*. Atglen, Pennsylvania: Schiffer Publishing, Ltd. 2001.

Beddinger, Margery. *Indian Silver: Navajo and Pueblo Jewelers*. Albuquerque, New Mexico: University of New Mexico Press. 1973.

Bell, Barbara, Ed Bell, and Steve Bell; and Ralph and Jerry McQueary, . *Zuni: The Art and the People, Vol. 2*. Grants, New Mexico: Squaw Bell Traders.1976.

Bell, Barbara, Ed Bell, and Steve Bell; and Ralph and Jerry McQueary. *Zuni: The Art and the People Vol. 3.* Grants, New Mexico: Squaw Bell Traders.1976.

Bulow, Ernie. [Beautiful Balancing Act: A Century of Olla Maidens." *Gallup Journey,* August 2010. pp. 20-22, Gallup, New Mexico: Gallup Journey Magazine. 2010.

Bunzel, Ruth L. *Zuni Kachinas: An Analytical Study,* Glorieta, New Mexico: The Rio Grande Press Inc., 1984.

Harmsen, Bill, Ed. *Patterns and Sources of Zuni Kachinas*. The Harmsen Publishing Company. 1988.

King, Dale Stuart. *Indian Silver Vol. II*. Tucson, Arizona: Dale Stuart King. 1976.

Ostler, James, Marian Rodee, and Milford Nahohai. *Zuni: A Village of Silversmiths*. Zuni, New Mexico: Zuni Ashiwi Publishing. 1996.

Ray Manley Photography. *Ray Manlay's Southwestern Indian Arts & Crafts.* Tucson, Arizona: Ray Manlay Photography, Inc. 1975.

Rosnek, Carl, and Jeseph Stacey. *Sky Stone and Silver. The Collector's Book of Southwest Indian Jewelry.* Englewood Cliffs, New Jersey: Prentice-Hall, Inc. 1977

Schaaf, Gergory. *American Indian Jewelry I.* Santa Fe, New Mexico: CIAC Press. 2003.

Schiffer, Nancy N. *Turquoise Jewelry.* Atglen, Pennsylvania: Schiffer Publishing, Ltd. 1990.

Schiffer, Nancy N. *Jewelry by Southwest American Indians: Evolving Designs.* Atglen, Pennsylvania: Schiffer Publishing, Ltd. 1990.

Sei, Toshio. *Knifewing and Rainbow Man in Zuni Jewelry.* Atglen, Pennsylvania: Schiffer Publishing, Ltd. 2010.

Slaney, Deborah C. *Blue Gem, White Metal: Carvings and Jewelry from the C. G. Wallace Collection.* Phoenix, Arizona: Heard Museum. 1998.

Sotheby Park Bernet. *The C. G. Wallace Collection of American Indian Art.* 1975.

Stevenson, Matilda Coxe. "The Zuni Indians: Their Mythology, Esoteric Fraternities and Ceremonies." *Twenty-Third Annual Report of the Bureau of American Ethnology to the Secretary of the Smithsonian Institution 1901-1902,* J. W. Powell, Ed. Washinton, DC: Government Printing Office. 1904.

Walsh, Barry. "Kikmongwi As Artist: The Katsina Dolls of Wilson Tawaquaptewa," *American Indian Art Magazine*, Winter 1998, pp. 52-59, Scotsdale, Arizona: American Indian Art, Inc., 1998.

Webb, William, and Robert A. Weinstein. *Dwellers at the Source: Southwestern Indian Photographs of A. C. Vroman, 1895-1904*. Albuquerque, New Mexico: University of New Mexico Press. 1973.

Wright, Barton. *Kachinas of the Zuni.* Flagstaff, Arizona: Northland Press.1985.

Wright, Barton. *Hallmarks of the Southwest.* Atglen, Pennsylvania: Schiffer Publishing, Ltd., 2000.

Artist Index

Kenneth Begay, 25
Shirley Benn, 24, 53, 130, 140, 146, 151
Virgil Benn, 53, 140, 146, 151
Edward Beyuka, 14, 18, 19, 31, 36, 37, 43, 91, 92, 94, 103, 105, 113, 116, 121, 122, 127, 130, 131, 157
Jonathan Beyuka, 43
Madeline Beyuka, 18, 24, 104, 105, 120, 122
Adrian Bowannie, 141
Jose Bowannie, 13, 126
Sybil Cachini, 18, 60, 61, 62, 71, 77
Delfina Cachini, 117
Robert Cachini, Sr., 18, 19, 60, 61, 62, 69, 70, 71
Olivia Panteah Calavaza, 51
Ronnie Calavaza, 51, 52
Rosary Calavaza, 33
Angela Cellicion, 18, 20
Dexter Cellicion, 18, 34, 35, 39, 40, 41, 44, 47, 56, 57, 58, 59, 74, 75, 76, 82, 83, 84, 85, 86, 109, 112, 157

Eva Cellicion, 19, 59, 74
Mary Ann Cellicion, 19, 84, 85, 86, 112
Oliver Cellicion, 19
Roger Cellicion, 56, 87
Rosemary Cellicion, 19, 82, 83
Charles Chuyate, 13
Harry Deutsawe, 6
Andrew Dewa, 19, 20, 32, 37, 57, 65, 66, 68, 69, 141, 142, 146, 157
Don Dewa, 19
Leekya Deyuse, 25
Duane Dishta, 73
Jerry Dixon, 21
Anthony Edaakie, 13, 20, 63, 64
Bradley Edaakie, 6, 13, 20
Dennis Edaakie, 19, 24
Margaret Edaakie, 19, 22
Merle Edaakie, 19, 32
Patty Zunie Edaakie, 26
Raylan Edaakie, 6, 20
Rita Edaakie, 6, 13, 20, 63, 64
Theodore Edaakie, 13, 19, 95, 96, 144
Beverly Etsate, 52, 72
Charlotte Eustace, 24
Philander Gia, 8, 45, 146, 147, 148, 149, 150

Anna Rita Homer, 6, 8, 15, 16, 17, 117, 118, 134, 135, 136
Fabian Homer, 92
Juana Homer, 6
Juanita Homer, 20
Lambert Homer, Jr., 8, 16, 17, 20, 91, 117, 118, 134, 135, 136
Lambert Homer, Sr., 13, 17, 20, 22, 34, 91
Raphael Homer, Jr., 6, 15
Alonzo Hustito, 25, 67
Erma Hustito, 25
Lapelle Kallestewa, 20
Mary Kallestewa, 20, 123, 124, 125, 157
Quanita Kallestewa 18
Curtis Kucate, 6, 21, 117, 118, 135
Theodore Kucate, 21
Elsie Laconsello, 16
Fred Laconsello, 16
Larry Laiwaate, 97
Morris "Red" Leekela, 21, 38, 41
Nicholas Leekela, 13
Sarah Leekya, 6
Faye Lonjose, 24
Leonard Lonjose, 21, 67, 136, 137, 138
Mabel Lonjose, 21, 22, 118, 119
Cecillia Licio, 107, 108

John Lucio, 14, 21, 97, 98, 99, 107, 108, 109, 115, 116, 121, 122, 129, 130, 131, 132, 146, 157
Paul Luna, 52
Vera Luna, 22, 40, 66, 139, 140
Jack Mahkee, 119
Eldred Martinez, 90, 91, 155, 156
Leonard Martza, 6, 19, 22, 28, 42, 89
Preston Monongye, 15
Mary Morgan, 23, 24
Walter Nahktewa (Nakatewa), 13, 22, 42, 68, 123, 126, 157
Josephine Nahohai, 25
Milford Nahohai, 6, 25
Randy Nahohai, 6
Daisy Nampeyo, 11, 13, 24, 128, 129
Delfine Nastacio, 117
Betty Natachu, 18, 22
Tony Ohmsatte, 22, 138, 139
Esther Panteah, 67
Martin Panteah, 67
Quincy Panteah, 23
Marcus Peyketewa, 6
Quincy Peynetsa, 23, 33, 111
Quintus Peynetsa, 23

Augustine Pinto, 23, 32, 47, 49, 50, 51, 52, 143
Rosalie Pinto, 23, 32, 50, 51, 52, 143
Ida Vacit Poblano, 23, 24, 26, 27, 46
Leo Poblano, 11, 14, 22, 23, 24, 26, 34, 43, 45, 53, 68, 91, 109, 111, 115, 121, 122, 123, 126, 127, 128, 129, 146, 157
Sam Poblano, 13, 109
Veronica Poblano, 23, 24
Charlie Poncho, 101, 102
Mary Ann Poncho, 101, 102
Elliott Qualo, 24, 133, 134
Ralph Quam, 24, 110
Octavius Seowtewa, 6
Dixon Shebola, 25, 48, 99, 100, 114
Martha Hustito Shebola, 25, 48
Lorandina Sheche, 6
Thelma Sheche, 6
Ann Sheyka, 25
Porfilio Sheyka, 24, 25, 80, 81
Andrea Lonjose Shirley, 82, 87, 88, 151, 152, 153, 154, 155

Dan Simplicio, 79
Dan Simplicio, Jr., 6
Tawaquaptewa, 14
Edith Tsabetsaye, 21, 136, 137, 138
Roger Tsabetsaye, 6
Genevieve Tucson, 6
Lee Tucson, 25
Myra Tucson, 25, 29, 30, 73, 90
Bessie Vacit, 6, 26
Elizabeth Leekya Vacit, 25
Frank Vacit, 22, 23, 30, 33, 55, 75, 76, 78, 79, 80, 7, 88, 92, 93, 133, 141, 142, 157
Gary Vacit, 26
Homer Vacit, 25
Jovanna Vacit, 25
Jerry Watson, 11, 13
Teddy Weahkee, 13
Tom Weahkee, 53
Lee Weebothee, 24
Mary Weebothee, 24
Linda Hustito Wheeler, 25
Ike Wilson, 23
Bruce Zunie, 11, 78
Geneva Zunie, 106
Helen Zunie, 26, 105
Joe Zunie, 26, 143, 145
Lincoln Zunie, 26, 105
William Zunie, 26, 106
Willie Zunie, 26